No frills guide to
Hiking in Mexico

No frills guide to
Hiking in Mexico

Jim Conrad

with Steven Vale
and other contributors

BRADT PUBLICATIONS

First published in 1992 by Bradt Publications, 41 Nortoft Rd, Chalfont St Peter, Bucks SL9 0LA, England. Distributed in North America by ITM Publishing, 736A Granville St, Vancouver B.C., V6Z 1G5, Canada.

British Library Cataloguing-in-Publication data

A catalogue record for this book is
available from the British Library

Cover by Mineli Laird
Illustrations by Jim Conrad
Maps by Patti Taylor
Typeset from the author's disc by Patti Taylor, London NW8 ORJ
Printed in Great Britain by BPCC Wheatons Ltd, Exeter

ACKNOWLEDGEMENTS

Jim Conrad thanks Joe Bowbeer for suggesting hikes.

Steven Vale wishes to thank Sue Kaesgen, who is studying Mayan textiles in Cleveland, and was a great companion in the mountain villages of Chiapas as were Lia Willebrand and Samuel Seward from Texas. Brenda and Ruthger (Holland) were amusing colleagues on both Popo and La Malinche and thanks should also go to Christine Frei (Switzerland), Monique, Margriet and Grace (NL), all volunteers at Na Balom, for help with digging out maps. Special thanks to Monique for accompanying me on the Chamal hike. Chip Morris (author of *The Living Maya*) and now actively involved in Biosphere Reserves, was a great source of knowledge on Chiapas as was Ignacio March of ECOSFERA. Also, a million thanks to Hilda Eeman (NL) for accompanying me on a gruelling Mexican tour. Finally, thanks are also due to Ronald Johnson and Ann-Marie Mackler in New Mexico for providing a welcome resting place and to Jonathan Theobald for allowing me to take his portable computer to Holland where much of the information was compiled.

Mexico: Location Map

Chapter 7: BAJA CALIFORNIA

1 La Bufadora
2 Camalú to El Rosario
3 Santa Rosalillita
4 Cedros Island
5 Laguna San Ignacio
6 Todos Santos
7 Between Loreto and Mulegé
8 Bahía de Los Ángeles
9 Puertecitos
10 Sierra San Pedro Mártir
11 Cataviña
12 Loreto to San Javier
13 San Francisco de la Sierra
14 Todos Santos/Sierra Laguna

Chapter 8: THE COPPER CANYON AREA

15 Copper Canyon
16 Cascada de Basaseachic

Chapter 9: OTHER DESTINATIONS IN NORTHERN MEXICO

17 El Salto to La Ciudad
18 Tamán to Xilitla
19 Peña Nevada

Chapter 10: CENTRAL MEXICO'S VOLCANOS

20 Volcán el Paricutín
21 Popocatépetl and Ixtaccíhuatl
22 Malinche
23 Volcán de Colima National Park

Chapter 11: YUCATÁN

24 Celestún Wildlife Refuge
25 Hormiguero/Río Bec Ruins
26 Hochob Ruin
27 Cobá Ruin

Chapter 12: CHIAPAS

28 San Cristóbal
29 Lagunas de Montebello
30 Cascades of Agua Azul
31 Volcán de El Chichonal
32 Palenque Ruins
33 Bonampak

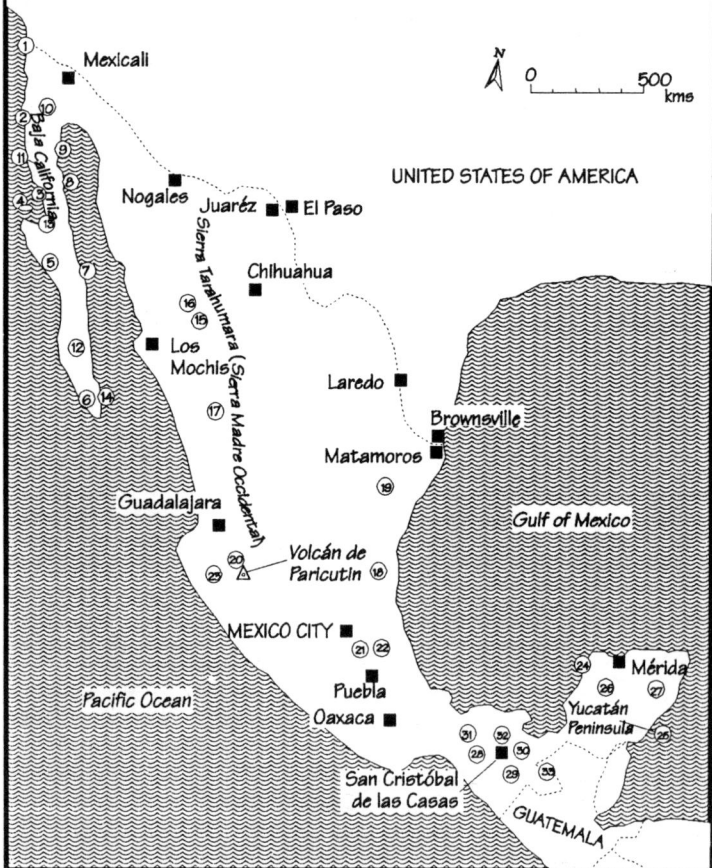

Mexicali

Baja California

UNITED STATES OF AMERICA

Nogales Juaréz El Paso

Sierra Tarahumara (Sierra Madre Occidental)

Chihuahua

Los Mochis

Laredo

Brownsville

Matamoros

Guadalajara

Gulf of Mexico

Volcán de Paricutín

MEXICO CITY

Pacific Ocean

Puebla

Oaxaca

Mérida

Yucatán Peninsula

San Cristóbal de las Casas

GUATEMALA

0   500 kms

CONTENTS

Part One: General Information

Part Two: The Hikes

SPECIAL INFORMATION BOXES

BRADT PUBLICATIONS

41 Nortoft Road, Chalfont St. Peter, Bucks., SL9 0LA, England

LETTER FROM THE PUBLISHER

Dear Readers

Like the best Mexican dishes, this book uses two main ingredients plus sprinklings of other flavours. Jim Conrad and Steven Vale provided the bulk of the book but there are some tastes of my 1982 *Backpacking in Mexico and Central America*: mostl˙ natural history, Indians and fiestas, and other bits and pieces. Jim, as editor (or chief cook, if you want to continue the metaphor) has stirred it all together.

The joy of the No Frills series is that by printing the book in small quantities it is easy to correct and update on a regular basis. If you find any inaccuracies (heaven forbid!) or have discovered some new hikes, do write. I would particularly like to include more maps. Your name will appear in print and you will earn my undying gratitude so it is well worth the effort!

I look forward to hearing from you.

Vaya con Dios,

Hilary Bradt

Part One

General Information

Chapter 1

Preparations

GETTING THERE CHEAPLY

In Britain Journey Latin America (JLA) sell cheap flights to Mexico. Phone 081-747 3108. An alternative for Europeans is to fly to Miami or Dallas/Ft. Worth, and then take Aeromexico to Mérida in the Yucatán, or Mexico City. Often it's even cheaper to look for the most inexpensive flight to *anywhere* in the U.S., and then take a Greyhound bus from there to the Mexican border, and continue traveling inside Mexico by buses. Your travel agent will know about special Greyhound tickets available to Europeans. Along the U.S./ Mexican border Greyhound stations are rarely an unreasonable hiking distance from a crossing point.

Even for North Americans Greyhound is usually the cheapest way to reach the border. Except during peak travel seasons, Greyhound usually offers special rates to U.S. travelers able to buy their tickets in advance. In 1992, for instance, a ticket purchased three weeks in advance is half-price, so that a one-way ticket from Kentucky to Mexico, a distance of 1,700km (1,000mi) costs about US$75.)

CLIMATE AND WHEN TO GO

Seasonal variations, drastic altitudinal changes, rainy and dry seasons, and the periodic weather system known as El Niño all conspire to create interesting if not rambunctious Mexican weather.

Northern Mexico's weather patterns often parallel those across the border in the U.S.; in January sometimes snow flurries occur along the border. Occasionally during the northern winter northern Mexico endures periods of two weeks or more of drizzly, windy, bone-chilling weather. During the northern winter even the Yucatán can experience nights so cold that you wouldn't want to be stuck in a beachside hammock at Playa del Carmen without a good sleeping bag. The Mexican highlands are usually cool or downright cold, even during the northern summer. Of course, during the northern hemisphere's summer, all of low-elevation Mexico is scorching.

In general, the rainy season occurs from about June through September and the dry season is from around January to April. During the rainy season, mornings usually begin clear and dewy-crisp, become progressively hotter and more humid, clouds start forming in mid morning, and then in the early afternoon, while the air is oppressively hot and humid, storm-clouds pop up on the horizon; usually it isn't long until one rolls right over you, drastically cooling things off and dramatically dumping huge amounts of rain. On an August afternoon after a big rain in Mexico City, you may be glad you brought along your thermal underwear.

El Niño is the name of a sporadic weather system occurring when a transient body of warm water invades the Pacific's usually chilly waters off Mexico's western coast. When you hear that this has happened (it comes every five to fifteen years, or so), you'd do well to reconsider any backpacking plans for northern Mexico — which includes Baja and the Copper Canyon area. El Niño causes one impulse of cold, rainy weather after the other to march across northern Mexico, turning vast saguaro and yucca deserts into veritable lakes. Southern Mexico and the Yucatán remain fairly unaffected. Actually, during recent years weather all over the world has been acting crazy, so don't depend too much on any of the above generalizations.

MONEY MATTERS

Mexico isn't as inexpensive as it used to be, but if after backpacking for a couple of weeks you hit a major city wanting to be pampered for a day or two, you can wreck a perfectly good budget. Traveler's checks can be cashed in most Mexican banks. U.S. dollars are always easy to change, even in out-of-the-way places. If you find yourself in a small town without a bank, or on a weekend when banks are closed, or if you just want to see if you can sell your dollars for a better rate than that being offered in the bank, usually you can find a local businessman happy to exchange. Hardware-store owners in small towns seem especially receptive to the idea; hotel and restaurant owners also are good.

Usually money changers on the U.S. side of the border give a few more pesos for the dollar than do Mexican banks. On the U.S. side, money exchanges are often available in odd nooks and crannies along streets near the crossing, and are often announced by hand-written signs reporting the current rate of exchange. Though you feel vulnerable dealing with such ad-hoc setups, I've never had any trouble using such places. Even in Mexican banks dollars are easier to exchange than traveler's checks. With traveler's checks, for validation purposes, you must often stand in one long line after the other, but with greenbacks usually waiting in just one line will do. For pure convenience, flexibility and dependability, nothing beats a money belt stuffed with $50 bills.

Before arriving in Mexico you might want to figure out a procedure for having money wired to you in case an emergency arises. Ask your own bank how this is done, and try to acquire a list of Mexican banks to which they will wire money. All over Mexico, in large bus stations, airports and in little offices along streets, public faxing offices have been established, so faxing may be the cheapest, fastest and easiest way to send an SOS back home; but be sure to bring along a number you can fax to.

Despite accommodation in Mexico being considerably more expensive than it is farther south in Central America, it's still possible to survive in Mexico fairly cheaply. Arriving in Mazatlán, if you want a room facing the beach, in a hotel with romantic grillwork around the windows, a sidewalk cafe in front, and snooty waiters speaking English, you'll pay U.S. prices or higher. But walk three blocks inland and next to the bus station you'll find the Hotel Economica, with a taco stand next to the entrance, a manager who doesn't speak a word of English, and double rooms with hot water for only US$10.

It's the same with food. If in a fancy restaurant in Mérida you order the legendary regional specialty called *huevos motuleños* (a scrumptious breakfast of layers of black beans, ham and fried eggs on crisp tortillas, topped with a spicy red sauce), you'll pay handsomely. On the other hand, if you find a mom-and-pop operation on a dusty side-street, you can enjoy a robust meal of eggs scrambled with onion, tomato, garlic and chili, black beans, rice and tortillas, with coffee, for less than US$3. In small towns and roadside *comedores*, often the meal costs half that. It's even cheaper to buy fruit in markets and tortillas by the kilo in *tortillarías*. Though it'd be a shame to miss the cuisine offered in Mexico's fancy restaurants, if you're just interested in maintaining a certain calorific intake to maintain the body while hiking, you can get along on US$1.50/day.

WHAT TO BRING

Apart from backpacking equipment, which is dealt with later, much of this is a question of personal preference. However, since inexperienced travelers tend to bring too much, we can give you some hints on how to cut down. Your pack shouldn't weigh more than about 18kg (40lb).

Clothes

Instead of carrying bulky items for colder temperatures, bring clothes that can be layered atop one another. Tee shirts are light but expose you to sunburn; a couple of cotton, long-sleeved shirts with pockets will protect you not only from sunburn but also insects and thieves. Trousers should be made from lightweight cotton or cotton-mix material and have deep, properly secured pockets (you can add these yourself). Jeans aren't suitable — they're heavy, hot, hard to wash, and take ages to dry. Two pairs of lightweight slacks weigh the same and are far more practical.

Women will be cool and comfortable in a dress or skirt (but bear in mind the problems of getting to your money belt if you're wearing a dress). You will need one thin woollen sweater, and another warmer one if you plan to hike up volcanoes. These, in addition to a lightweight windproof jacket, should keep you warm enough, although thermal underwear takes up little room and is excellent in very cold conditions. Don't forget rain gear. Rubber thongs or flip-flops are good for hot weather, though if you wear them in some places you might get hookworms; people with small feet can buy them inexpensively almost anywhere in Mexico. Sneakers are nice, though if you hike in them, spines from Mexico's many species of well-armored trees will easily penetrate their soles, and your feet.

In hot, humid climates, towels are hard to dry and easily become corrupted with mildew. Instead of towels, consider taking several large, easy-to-dry bandannas.

Don't forget your swimsuit. In coastal tourist areas with coral reefs offshore, as at Playa del Carmen, masks, snorkels and even air tanks can be rented; if you plan to camp along isolated shores you might want to bring your own mask and snorkel.

A hat is essential. Straw ones for small heads can be purchased in any Mexican town, but cotton ones are nice because on long, hot hikes, when you pass a stream, you can fill the hat with water, plonk it on your head and then, as the water evaporates, your head will be *cool*!

What You Need to Know about Sun Glasses

by Dr. Bob Vinton

Too much sunlight increases risks of cataracts. Here are some points to keep in mind when shopping for sunglasses:

— sunglasses should be so dark you can't see your eyes in the mirror

— the ability to absorb UV radiation, which damages the eyes, is not determined by lens color or darkness; buy sunglasses advertised to block 95% to 100% of UVB rays and at least 60% of UVA rays

— glass lenses are heavier than plastic ones, but are much more scratch resistant; materials such as "Lexan polycarbonate," "CR-39," "Carbonite 360," "Malenium 99," and "Plutonite" are just plastic

— check for lens distortion by moving your head up and down and side to side while looking at a rectangular design; if there are no distortions, the rectangle's sides won't bow in and out

— gray and green lenses distort colors least; brown-amber improve contrast in haze or fog but cause other color distortions

— mirror lenses are no better against UV than ordinary lenses

— polarized lenses reduce reflected glare off glass and water but have nothing to do with UV protection

— the best sunglasses are large, curved to fit the face and are fitted with opaque or UV-blocking side-shields

— wearing a broad-brimmed hat with ordinary sunglasses can reduce UV exposure to the eyes by 95%

Other Useful Items

Here's a checklist from which you can pick and choose: a small flashlight (torch), with spare bulb, traveler's alarm-clock, penknife (preferably Swiss Army type), sewing kit, safety pins, large needles and strong thread for tent repairs, scissors, Scotch tape (Sellotape), pencils and ball-point pens, a small notebook for names and addresses, a large notebook for your diary and letters home, plastic bags (the 'zip-loc' type are the most useful), a plug for baths and sinks (the flat rubber sort that fits everything or — even better — a squash ball), plastic clothesline, clothespins (pegs), small scrubbing brush, laundry soap (bought in Mexico), shampoo, soap (liquid soap), toilet roll, dental floss (excellent for doing running repairs as well as teeth), earplugs (a godsend in noisy hotels and on night buses), spare glasses and contact lenses, sunglasses (see box), binoculars, spare passport photos, rubber band to hold together your passport with other documents inside it, insect repellent,

Spanish dictionary and phrase book, pocket calculator and, finally, an extra, lightweight, nylon bag with a zipper — you can leave things locked in it in your hotel when you're out hiking.

APPEARANCE

It's always been inadvisable to dress outlandishly in Latin America; officials sometimes treat travelers who look dirty and penniless with suspicion and contempt, and if you look like a drug addict (in their eyes) you can bring all kinds of problems onto yourself. So shortish hair and trimmed beards for men and reasonably conventional clothing for women are sensible.

Small-town, rural Mexico is conservative and Catholic, and many Mexicans in these areas consider wearing shorts and going braless in public as offensive. Even in (especially in) more cosmopolitan areas, women risk inviting comments and unworthy behavior from all those macho men. If you're a woman preferring going without a bra because it's cooler, you'll find that a man's shirt with breast pockets (!) handily obscures your femininity.

After traveling a while you'll discover certain spots especially favored by alternative-type travelers who run around in the most provocative states of dress and undress — even beaches where everyone is naked — and you may feel a powerful urge to join in. Use your common sense in such situations, and always remember that just because others are doing something, that doesn't make it right. Nudity is, in fact, illegal. Mexico belongs to the Mexicans; we're guests there, and we shouldn't impose our mores onto our hosts.

Though Mexico is one of the most stable of all Latin countries, it's not a good idea to wear camouflage patterns. Never wear army-style shirts with epaulets. Some go as far as to eschew khaki, but others wear it with no problem.

PHOTOGRAPHY

For snapshot-type photography there are plenty of "35mm compact auto-focus cameras" to choose from. Serious backpacking photographers, however, always face the dilemma that they need heavy lenses and tripods, while also needing to keep their pack light. Therefore, before you go you need to decide unequivocally how high photography stands on your list of priorities. If it's low, then something like a Fuji FZ-5, which sells for about US$30, will do. If it's high, then be prepared to carry a heavy pack, and to upgrade your watchfulness several notches, to ward off theft.

If you're content with excellent snapshots of people and scenes, a standard 50mm lens will suffice. But if you want pictures of leaf-cutter ants carrying their leaf-tatter parasols, or closeups of hibiscus blossoms, you'll need a macro lens. If you know what you're doing, using lightweight extension tubes or reversal rings will be lighter and less expensive than carrying a regular macro. Unless you're serious about getting bird shots, or taking unobtrusive, long-distance people-pictures, the extra weight makes carrying a good telephoto lens undesirable. One option is to get a telephoto lens that focuses close enough to serve as a macro — though you may lose some macro quality with it.

Especially if you plan to photograph in the forest, lighting becomes a critical problem. For proper depth of field, even if you use a fast film such as ISO/ASA 400, really you need a tripod. Remember that the higher your F-number, the greater your depth of field (the more in focus); if in a forest you shoot at F 22, maybe 90% will be in focus, but if you shoot at F 1.2 so that you can use a faster shutter-speed, 90% may be out of focus. In dense forest, flashes can be a great help. Usually when you see a pretty fern, mushroom, turtle or frog in the forest, there's simply not enough light for a good shot, unless you use a tripod or a flash.

If there's a possibility that someday you might want to sell your pictures to a magazine, or give programs at schools, then shoot color slides, not prints. If you really want sharp pictures that can be "blown up," probably you'll find ISO/ASA-400 film too grainy; ISO/ASA 125 or 100 gives excellent results, though you'll need more light, which translates into diminished depth of field for any given shutter speed.

Bring film with you. Usually what you buy in Mexico is fine, but sometimes what's available has been subject to high temperatures or some other emulsion-unfriendly situation.

DOCUMENTS

All tourists need a Tourist Card, valid for 90 days and issued free by Mexican consulates. It is usually, but not always, available at the border.

A special note for U.S. citizens: Though it's true that legally all you need is a tourist card (no passport), it's also true that sometimes Mexican soldiers and officials unaccustomed to U.S. tourists find it highly suspicious that an anglo would be traveling with only a flimsy piece of paper, which is what the Mexican tourist card amounts to. Also, if later you might cross back to the U.S. looking sunburned, dusty and skin-scratched, or if you speak English with a peculiar accent or have a non-white skin color, U.S. Customs might give you special attention. The last four times I crossed into Texas from Mexico I was pulled aside by U.S. customs officials, had his passport run through the computer, my backpack searched, researched, and sniffed by dogs, my camera lenses and binoculars peered through (no dope inside them), and generally made to feel culpable of unspeakable crimes. ("What's that I *smell*, sir?" "Sweaty socks and sour tortillas... ?") At times like that, the dear passport enhances one's sense of security.

Anona (custard apple)

Chapter 2

Health and Safety

HEALTH
by Dr. Bob Vinton

Immunizations

No immunizations are required for entering Mexico, but "Don't forget your shots" still is good advice — especially for anyone visiting the Mexican outback. Backpackers should consider immunization against tetanus, typhoid, polio and measles. There is now a highly effective vaccine against Hepatitis A, available in Britain but not yet in the USA.

The Basic First-Aid Kit

Anyone trying for a light backpack will shudder at the idea of carrying items like scalpels and hypothermia thermometers. However, each component of the following list deserves serious consideration:

Bandage Materials

Absolute essentials are marked with an asterisk.
adhesive pads (Band-Aids, plasters) for minor cuts and scrapes
butterfly closure bandages to pull together skin around deep cuts
gauze pads for large wounds
adhesive tape and *bandage material* to hold large pads in place
elastic bandages for securing dressings or wrapping sprains

moleskin or *molefoam* for blisters
splints for fractures

Instruments

#11 scalpel blade with handle
tweezers for cactus spines
small scissors
oral thermometer
hypothermia thermometer
surgical tubing or *bandanna* for constricting band
sling/ triangular bandage
instructions for performing CPR (cardiopulmonary resuscitation)
snakebite kit with a suction device

Medications

aspirin and/or tylenol (Paracetamol) and/or ibuprofen
antacid tabs
antihistamine-decongestant tabs
antibiotic ointment
cavit or other temporary dental filling
chloroquine for malarial zones
steroid ointment or cream for insect bites, allergic rashes
diamox for high altitude sickness
oral rehydration salt packets for diarrhea, dehydration
Immodium for diarrhea
Pepto-Bismol tablets for diarrhea
throat lozenges

Other Items

insect repellent
insect sting kit if allergic to stings
lip balm with sunscreen
sunscreen rated at SPF #15 or greater
iodine or water purification pills

Selected Diseases and Emergencies

Traveler's Diarrhea

Boil it, cook it, peel it or forget it! Traveler's diarrhea (Montezuma's revenge) results from ingesting contaminated food or water. Especially risky foods include raw vegetables, meat and seafood, tap

The Dehydration Problem

When you're dehydrated the body has problems circulating blood and regulating body temperature. The decreased circulation hampers oxygen and nutrient flow to the brain, resulting in fatigue, cramping muscles, irritability, headaches, disorientation and impaired judgment. Average adults need at least 2-3 liters (2-3qt) of liquid a day to replace normal losses.

You can become dehydrated without noticing it; the human "thirst mechanism" isn't very sensitive and if backcountry hikers depend on it they'll probably fall behind in fluid replacement especially at altitude or if you are ill. Therefore, it's very important to take fluid according to a schedule rather than perceived thirst. Prior to leaving camp in the morning, "hyperhydrate" yourself by drinking 25-50ml (8-16oz) of liquid, preferably non-alcoholic. During moderate to heavy outdoor activity at hot temperatures, drink 30-50ml (10-16oz), even if not thirsty. Properly hydrated, you should pee ½ to 1 liter (½ to 1qt) every day.

If you become seriously dehydrated from diarrhea or some other cause, it's possible that the electrolytes in your body will need to be replaced. A **simple rehydration solution** consists of one heaped teaspoon of sugar and a large pinch (¼ teaspoon) of salt in a glass (⅓ pint) of water. Drink one glass every time the bowels are opened.

Salt tablets should be avoided because they markedly increase the body's water requirement.

water, ice, salsa, unpeeled fruit, mayonnaise and unpasteurized dairy products, expecially ice cream. Pepto-Bismol seems to prevent some cases of diarrhea. Take two tablets with meals and at bedtime during the risky period (but not to exceed 21 days).

Once you have diarrhea, avoid all solid foods, dairy products, caffeine-containing beverages, alcohol and citrus juices. To prevent dehydration, drink copious amounts of fluids — sips if you feel sick. Once the diarrhea ends, begin eating clear soups such as chicken or vegetable broths, and graduate to soft foods such as applesauce and cooked rice. Clear soups are OK during diarrhea although very hot and very cold foods induce reflex emptying of the bowel.

Sometimes recovery can be hastened by taking two Pepto-Bismol tablets every 30 minutes for eight doses, along with Immodium (Loperamide) in the suggested dosage. Two double-strength Septra or Bactrim tablets along with Immodium tablets can stop diarrhea within one hour in some cases. However, because of increased resistance to Septra in Mexico the new antibiotics norfloxacin or ciprofloxacin are more effective, although more expensive. Antibiotics may need to be continued for 3 days or more. If serious dehydration, persistent fever, or bloody stools develop, contact a physician. Most prescription medications, except for narcotics, can be bought over the counter in Mexico.

Insect Repellents

The best all-purpose insect repellent, according to the U.S. Dept. of Agriculture, is diethyltoluamide, commonly called "Deet." Other good repellents include ethyl hexanedial and dimethyl phthalate. No repellent is active against stinging insects such as ants, bees and wasps. Most repellents remain effective from one to three hours, but can be removed sooner by rain, bathing, swimming, sweating or wiping. For ticks and chiggers apply to tops of shoes and around openings in clothing. Insect repellents shouldn't be applied to damaged skin such as skin with sunburn or dermatitis.

Deet used in at least 30% concentration is recommended. The 3M Company has a special 31% Deet cream formulation called Ultrathon, which provides 12 hours of protection and is water resistant. Deet is absorbed through the skin and into the blood. Toxic and allergic reactions have been reported, especially in children and infants. Avoid contact with synthetic plastic surfaces, such as eyeglass frames and synthetic fabrics.

Since using chemicals effectively as bug repellents can clearly have some side-effects, here are some common-sense alternatives to replace or reduce chemical-repellent use:

- use pyrethrum-containing insect sprays on clothing (not on skin) and in sleeping areas (pyrethrum is natural and organic)
- use mosquito coils (incense-like items that burn slowly, giving off fumes that drive away mosquitos)
- stay in screened areas after sunset and sleep inside a mosquito net
- wear long-sleeve shirts and full-length pants
- wear light-colored clothing (dark attract mosquitoes)
- avoid perfume, after-shave lotion, and scented soaps
- don't go barefoot or wear open sandals
- sleep under a mosquito net.

Malaria

Malaria is endemic to much of lowland Mexico, particularly the southern regions, and it's on the increase. It's increasing because anopheles mosquitoes, which transmit the disease from one person to another, are becoming resistant to insecticides; also, the malaria microorganism itself is becoming resistant to traditional antimalarial drugs. Chloroquine is still the best antimalarial drug for traveling in Mexico's remote, high-risk areas. Check with your local public health department or travel clinic for current recommendations. In the U.S., the malarial hotline of the Center for Disease Control in Atlanta will give you the newest information on malaria, at (404) 332-4555 (in the UK tel: 071-388 9600 or 071-636 8636). Anyone developing recurrent fevers, sweats, malaise and headache during or following travel in malarial zones should obtain medical evaluation as soon as possible. One symptom of malaria is having fevers alternating with chills.

Cholera

Although in recent years cholera was not considered as much of a problem in Mexico, recently there have been sporadic, limited outbreaks in southern and central Mexico and the Juarez border area. Cholera is an acute intestinal infection caused by the bacteria *Vibrio cholera*, and is acquired by ingesting contaminated water or food; person-to-person transmission is rare. It usually occurs in epidemics where there is overcrowding, malnutrition and poor sanitation. The incubation period is from one to three days, and can be followed by voluminous, explosive diarrhea, with copious vomiting in severe cases. The liquid stool is gray, without fecal odor, and known as "rice-water stools." If these symptoms occur you should seek immediate medical attention and begin drinking oral rehydration salt solution. Tetracycline or Septra are the antibiotic treatments of choice. Travelers to cholera-infested areas should avoid uncooked food, and peel fruits or vegetables themselves. Carbonated bottled water and soft drinks are usually safe. Cholera vaccine affords only short-lived, limited protection and is not recommended for travel to Mexico. Cholera is not a very contagious disease and can be avoided by seeing that you always "boil it, cook it, peel it or forget it."

Intestinal Worms

If you see worms in your stool, a fresh stool sample should be taken directly to a medical lab in Mexico for examination. The other alternative is shotgun therapy with Mebendazole 100mg, taken morning and evening for three consecutive days (contra-indicated in pregnancy). That will rid you of most roundworm infections. Worms do no harm and you can wait for treatment until you get home.

Chagas Disease

I've never heard of anyone contracting this nasty-sounding malady,
transmitted by the barber bug, but since you get it by sleeping on
dirt floors frequented by opossums, readers of this book might be
more vulnerable than, say, a Fodor follower. Use a hammock if you
sleep in native huts.

Dengue fever

Dengue or breakbone fever is a viral infection occurring in epidemics
in Mexico's low-lying urban areas; it's transmitted by the *Aedes*
mosquito and in healthy adults is seldom fatal. Dengue begins 5-8
days after exposure with the sudden onset of high fevers, severe
aching of the head, back and extremities, sore throat and complete
exhaustion. A measles-like rash occurs 3-5 days after onset of fever.
It can mimic the flue or malaria. There is no treatment or vaccine
currently available, and antibiotics are of no use. Plenty of fluid
should be taken to prevent dehydration. Use Tylenol (Paracetemol),
not aspirin, for pain or fever. Japanese B encephalitis vaccine has
some protective effect.

Rabies

Apart from bats, especially vampire bats, dogs are the biggest
danger. The conventional advice is if bitten by a dog you should try
to catch it or locate its owner because it's important to know if the
animal subsequently dies of rabies, in which case you must start
treatment immediately.

A series of injections spaced over a period of three months will
prevent the disease which, once established, is invariably fatal.
However, Dr Jane Wilson comments, "Once the rabies virus enters
the body it migrates slowly along the nerves to the brain. Symptoms
will appear in about two weeks if the bite is to the face but may be
delayed as much as two years if the bite is on a foot. If you are
unsure whether the animal is rabid it may be safe to wait until you
return home before starting the course of injections."

If you plan to enter areas with an unusually high risk of rabies, a
vaccine is available.

Heat Exhaustion

If you've been over-exerting yourself in a hot area and you feel faint,
nauseous, you have a rapid, fluttery heartbeat, and especially if
you're pale and your skin is cold and clammy, you're probably

suffering from heat exhaustion. The condition is not dangerous, but it is a warning to rest in the shade, sip cool liquids, and munch a high-energy trail snack to avoid having a heat stroke.

Heat Stroke

Heat-stroke victims have a very high body temperature and skin that is hot, flushed and *dry*. If untreated, heat stroke can result in brain damage or even death. The treatment consists of bringing down the body's temperature by any means possible. Remove the victim's clothing and sponge him with water, then fan him vigorously. Massage his arms and legs to divert blood to his extremities. Continue this until his temperature is normal, and abandon the hike. If you continue, a recurrence is quite possible.

Fungus Infections

Fungi thrive in hot, humid places, and much of Mexico fits that description. Sprinkle a foot-powder such as Tinaderm or Mexana between your toes night and morning; keep your socks dry and change them frequently. If you develop a persistent and itchy, red rash, this could be a fungus that can be killed by use of antifungal creams such as clotrimazole 1% or miconazole 2%. Another type of fungus lives in tropical rivers and can infect the ears of bathers. Use ear-plugs and after swimming irrigate your ear canals with a solution of half vinegar and half isopropyl rubbing alcohol.

Prickly Heat (Miliaria)

This irritating rash is caused by the blocking of sweat glands. Loose-fitting, cotton clothes help prevent it; washing with cold water and a solution of soda bicarbonate will help clear it up. Use sunblock gel, not cream which will further clog the pores.

High-Altitude Sickness

This is caused by decreased atmospheric pressure, resulting in less oxygen being available to the lungs, blood and other tissues. In general, the symptoms include headache, light-headedness, nausea, loss of appetite, weakness, shortness of breath and insomnia beginning 6 to 48 hours after ascent.

Of course the best treatment is to descend to a lower elevation; even descending 300-600m (1,000-2,000ft) can ameliorate some symptoms. Taking oxygen is effective, but any trekker having problems should descend rather than wait for oxygen. Taking 500mg of Diamox (acetazolamide), a sulfa derivative, once a day in the morning can prevent or diminish symptoms; begin dosage one day prior to ascent, and continue for two or more days after ascent. Avoid alcohol and sleeping medications; a low-salt diet rich in carbohydrates may also stave off symptoms.

Sunburn

Remember that on bright, hazy or even cloudy days it's possible to receive 70% to 80% of a clear day's UV radiation — and UV is what causes sunburn. Prevent sunburn by using sunscreens. Mineral oils, creams and lotions lubricate and even change the skin's optical properties but do not protect from sunburn. There are two main kinds of sunscreen: reflectors and absorbers. Reflectors, such as zinc oxide and titanium dioxide, which are white pastes, reflect and scatter UV wavelengths; because they are thick and messy, reflectors are used only in high-risk areas such as the nose and lips. Absorber sunscreens such as PABA (para-aminobenzoic acid), cinnamates, benzophenones and parsol absorb UV waves. Sunscreens with high "sun protection factors" (SPF#) include Presun, Bullfrog, Supershade, Sundown, Tiscreen and Total Eclipse. Some sunscreens are water-resistant.

Soak mild to moderate sunburn in cold water and give ice massages. Take two adult aspirins every four hours. Solarcaine and other anesthetics that smear on are not recommended because allergic reactions can occur.

Severe sunburn with blisters should receive a physician's treatment. The deleterious effects of sun exposure are rough, sagging skin with liver spots, wrinkles, and increased skin-cancer risks. These effects are cumulative, irreversible, and begin at an early age. By the time wrinkles appear, the damage is done. Prevention is the name of the game.

Snakebite

Avoid snakebite by staying on the trail, watching your feet, and never putting your hands where you can't see them. Wear good boots and thick socks. Most snakes are active at night so move cautiously after dark and be sure your tent or hammock is snake-proof. Shake out your boots in the morning. Symptoms of having been bitten by a poisonous snake include bleeding at the bite, tingling in the mouth, and a metallic taste, followed by swelling and pain. Of the few people bitten by venomous snakes, only half receive any venom at all.

If bitten, place a constricting band, not a tourniquet, *lightly* about

5cm (2in) from the bite, between the bite and the body, and move it toward the body as swelling progresses. For about 30 minutes suck out the venom, either with a suction device or the mouth (assuming no sores or gum diseases afflict the mouth); empty the suction device every 5-10 minutes. If the bite is on an arm or leg, keep the extremity below the heart's level and immobilize. Give the victim copious amounts of *non-alcoholic* fluids. If alone, walk slowly and rest periodically while going for help. Electric shock or "stun guns" are useless. Keeping calm is crucial.

Never use ice or give antivenin in the field. Assume that every snakebite is a medical emergency and evacuate the victim as soon as possible.

Insect Bites and Stings

If stung by a honey bee, often the stinger remains behind; that should be removed as soon as possible by gently scraping sideways with a knife blade or stick. Small and large none-life-threatening bites and stings can be treated with ice, elevating the affected area, and by taking antihistamines such as Benadryl (Piriton or Triludon) (50mg every 8-12 hours), which may be bought over the counter.

Of course, people known to be especially allergic to stings should carry an insect sting kit containing epinephrine (adrenaline), and know how and when to use it. To lessen the possibility of stings and bites, wear long-sleeved shirts and long pants, and don't wear perfumes, scented deodorants or cosmetics. Wear subdued-colored, snug-fitting clothing. When confronted by stinging insects, back off.

Scorpion Stings

Scorpions are nocturnal and reclusive. They usually inhabit rotting trees, tree bark and palm trees, and they hide under rocks, and in the nooks and crannies of Indian huts. Only 8 of 25 scorpion species found in Mexico pose a serious threat to humans. The eight dangerous Centriroides species are called bark scorpions and are small, 2-3in in length with an elongated narrow constricted body. They can cause serious and even fatal systemic reactions, expecially in young children. Specific anti-venom is avilable in Arizona and Mexico for severe envenomation. Most scorpion-sting victims suffer only mild pain lasting less than four hours; mild analgesics and cold compresses or ice are all that is required. Use of the extractor suction device may be helpful.

Ticks (*Garrapatas*)

Keep ticks off your skin by tucking trousers into socks and by spraying clothing and your legs with a repellent; do the same with gaps around your midriff. Periodically inspect your body; some ticks are so small as to be practically invisible. At day's end, wash thoroughly (Neko soap, available in tick countries, is effective) and change your clothing. Once they've dug in, ticks must be removed with tweezers by grasping the tick head as close as possible to the skin and gently pulling — no jerking. If a rash appears, seek medical attention.

Chiggers

Chiggers are 1mm long red mites found in moist grassy or bushy areas. They feed on blood and tissues by piercing the skin and sucking. Their bites form welts which are accompanied by insufferable itching for up to 10 days. To avoid getting them, use lots of repellent and keep away from high grass. The itch can be relieved a little with an analgesic ointment or steroid cream.

Crabs and Lice

Budget travelers sleeping in cheap hotels are liable to catch these. Usually they are caught by close physical contact with infested people. If in your hair or pubic area, shampoo with something containing gamma benzene hexachloride or permethrin.

Jellyfish Stings

Most stings occur between July and September. Usually jellyfish stings are mild and symptoms disappear in 2 or 3 hours; a rash may persist for a few days. If a jellyfish's tentacles latch onto you, remove them preferably not with bare hands. Wash the affected area with cold salt water (Don't use fresh water and don't rub sand over the affected area). Soak the injured part in vinegar for about 30 minutes, then apply a paste of baking soda, wet sand or shaving cream, and leave in place for several minutes. Scrape off and wash with salt water. If itching is a problem, apply a steroid cream or Itch Balm Plus; an oral antihistamine such as Benadryl (Piriton which may make you drowsy, or Triludant) may help. If vinegar isn't available, use rubbing alcohol, bleach, distilled liquor, meat tenderizer or... urine.

Stingray Stings

Stingray are the most commonly encountered, venomous, marine animals. Avoid being stung by doing the "stingray shuffle" — that is, cause turbulence with your feet when walking in the water, to warn stingray that you're coming so they can swim away. When poking around in corals or going wading, wear protective gloves and shoes or booties. After being stabbed on the foot or leg by a well-camouflaged stingray you'll have to deal with both a laceration and an injection of venom. The sting causes immediate and intense local pain, swelling and bleeding that usually peaks in 30 to 60 minutes. Fragments of the stinger, or sheath, may be left behind and should be removed. Soak the affected area water as hot as you can stand it without burning for 30 to 90 minutes and repeat as necessary for relief of pain. Rinse the wound with water and bandage appropriately. If severe pain persists or if spines or stingers possibly remain in the wound, or if there is any evidence of infection, seek medical attention.

Disclaimer

The advice in this chapter is based on standard medical principles but is not intended to replace the advice of your own doctor.

SAFETY

Theft

Robberies often figure prominently in travelers' tales, and certainly Mexico has its share of skilful thieves. Fortunately, violent robbery is very rare and theft in rural areas is highly unlikely. Travelers are most likely to be parted from their possessions unknowingly, particularly in places frequented by tourists. Here are a few do's and don'ts:

Do keep your valuables in a money belt, neck pouch, or secret pocket. Zippered bags are useful — fasten them inside your slacks, around a leg, or deep within a backpack. This is a good place to hide such things as your passport, address book, plane ticket. John Hatt, in his excellent book *The Tropical Traveller*, suggests using Tubigrip to secure valuables to one's leg; tubigrip is an elasticized tube bandage coming in various sizes. Experiment with the most comfortable and practical place to wear it. Bear in mind that to be seen with your hand deep inside your trousers can be embarrassing.

Do bring a combination lock (harder to pick than an ordinary padlock) to secure your hotel door or luggage. If you're willing to carry the extra weight, a chain is a useful and versatile addition.

Do select hotel rooms with bars on the window, or one that can't be entered from a neighboring room. Don't carry a handbag or any type of shoulder bag into such known danger-spots as markets, fiestas, crowded buses and trains; leather bags are especially easy to snatch or slit.

Don't leave your money in your clothes when you go swimming.

Don't camp in urban areas unless they are well guarded.

Finally, **don't** become paranoid. Backpackers in rural areas experience incredible honesty and generosity in the face of grinding poverty. It's a humbling experience.

U.S. citizens in Mexico can comfortably carry their tourist cards with them. However, other travelers carrying bulky passports face the question of whether to carry the passport with them at all times or to leave it in a hotel strong box. If you do leave the passport behind, carry some other form of identification — something impressive-looking with a photo and a number will usually do. Maybe an International Youth Hostel card, or even a driver's license.

Always keep identification and a note of the numbers of your passport, plane ticket and travelers checks separate from your valuables so that if they are lost, you can more easily replace them.

Officials

You will be up against petty bureaucracy time and again, receiving free training in the art of public relations. However frustrating the situation, however corrupt the official, you must always remain calm and pleasant. Never do anything to threaten the fragile, macho-based ego of any official. Often a potentially awkward situation can be avoided with jokes and a friendly gesture, such as the offer of some chocolate.

Once bribery in Mexico was easy and almost compulsory. However, now the federal government is making a genuine effort to rid corruption from the system. This results in there being some officials still ensnaring travelers on trumped-up charges, with a view to receiving the famous *mordida* (the bite) to supplement their income, but other officials who become insulted if you try to bribe them. They'll accuse you of subverting the Mexican Revolution, and you'll be in a heap of trouble.

Chapter 3

Backpacking

INTRODUCTION

Some readers may be experienced travelers who have never backpacked, others may be experienced backpackers who have never traveled in a developing country. To both we say "Welcome!" The combination of backpacking and travel gives you the best of both worlds. The backpacker's self reliance enables him literally to walk away from the crowds and see scenery, wildlife and people that are inaccessible to other travelers, and the traveler's curiosity ensures that he enjoys them.

You can be a true explorer and wander at will with just a compass and map, climb volcanoes "because they're there" (and because the view from the top is superb), explore national parks and observe animals, or hike established trails through mountains and jungles, visiting small villages on the way. Even for regular travel you'll be much more flexible and comfortable than the average *gringo*, and you'll save money, too. When traveling by public transport the inevitable delays and breakdowns hold no fears when you can brew some tea and spread your sleeping bag outside, and of course you can economize all the way by cooking your own food and camping out instead of staying in hotels.

The growing number of well-managed national parks offer good hiking but much of the best hiking is away from national parks, in areas with a large Indian population where networks of trails link isolated villages. Planning hikes in many of these areas is difficult without good maps. Nearly always, however, if two villages are next to one another on a map, unless there's a big river, a very deep canyon with vertical walls, or a huge mountain between them, if there's no road, by asking around you'll be able to find an interesting trail connecting them....

If you haven't backpacked before we suggest you get some experience in your own country before hitting the Mexican trails.

EQUIPMENT AND SUPPLIES

Backpack

If you're buying a new pack for the trip, you should probably get one with an internal frame; external aluminum frames are easily broken, snag on every tree-limb, and project into awkward places when you're holding it or trying to store it away. On the other hand they are a lot cooler.

Sleeping Bag

The tropics are too humid for down to make an ideal filler — a very light artificial fiber is preferable. A "bivouac cover" or simply a plastic sheet or a poncho will add a lot of warmth at high altitudes and can be left behind when you're hiking in warmer areas. If you plan to climb the high volcanoes (Popo, Ixta etc) you should have a suitably warm bag.

Mat

Insulation and protection from the cold, hard ground can mean the difference between a good and a bad night of sleep. Closed-cell "ensolite" foam pads are most efficient, providing excellent insulation and tolerable padding, even when less than 1cm (2½in) thick. Possibly the best mat of all is a Thermarest, a combination of air mattress and foam pad. It's lightweight, compact, comfortable, and comes in two lengths — three-quarters and full.

Tent or Hammock

You'll probably need some sort of tent and it must be bugproof and waterproof. It should also be as light as possible — not more than 2.5kg (5½lb) for a two-man tent. Ventilation is important; if your tent is inadequate in this way, cut windows in the front and rear, and face them with mosquito netting. In fact, it's easy enough to make a tropical tent entirely out of mosquito netting, using tarpaulin as a fly!

Many people prefer a hammock to a tent for the humid, jungle areas. They are very comfortable, and often it's easier or preferable to find two trees suitably spaced than to clear an area for a tent. However, remember that two hammocks can weigh more than a light, two-man tent, and you must be able to rig up the netting so no insects can get inside. Excellent mesh hammocks can be bought in Mexico, especially in the Yucatán.

While on the subject, did you know that there's a right way and a wrong way to lie in a hammock? If instead of lying parallel with the hammock's sides (which forces your body to sag into a cramped U position), you lie diagonally (not perpendicularly) across it, your body and legs will remain more or less horizontal.

Boots

You don't need heavy boots for any of these hikes. Good ankle support and shock absorption are important, as are solid rubber soles capable of standing up to lava, tree-spines and long-term ordinary use. Needless to say, whatever you find most comfortable in the long run, use.

Stove

Jim Conrad finds stoves too heavy, bulky and messy to fool with; there's nothing wrong with carrying powdered milk, oatmeal, animal crackers, and buying fruits in *mercado* and occasionally eating in restaurants. However, travelers more gastronomically advanced, or if they suffer desperate addictions to morning caffeine, might need to carry one. Kerosene and white gas are usually available for backpacking stoves.

Pots and Pans

There's no need to spend a fortune buying special backpacker's lightweight saucepans. Perfectly suitable aluminum ones are sold throughout Mexico. Plastic plates and cups keep your food and drink hotter than metal ones. Bowls are more versatile than plates.

Trail Food

One excellent backpacking staple is packaged soups, but these can sometimes be hard to find in Mexico. Noodles add bulk to soup and provide a perfectly adequate trail meal. Oatmeal is available in most well-stocked Mexican supermarkets — it's called *avena*. Rice and dried beans are easy to find. During certain seasons roasted peanuts are abundant and inexpensive. One of the most delightful mysteries of Mexico is that nearly every supermarket sells a certain lightweight, high-energy, remarkably tasty, outrageously inexpensive food that stands up well on the trail — *animal crackers*! They usually cost less than a dollar a kilo (2.2lb); ask for *animalitos* — *las galletas dulces*. Of course, any diet in which animal crackers form a conspicuous component should be supplemented with vitamin pills, for there's not much redeeming about them other than their taste, quick energy, and cute shapes.

Other Items

Canteens (water flask), waterproof matches, waterproofing for boots, compass, nylon straps, plastic bags, and a large plastic garbage bag (bin liner) for covering your pack at night if left outside the tent (safe areas only).

HIKING IN THE RAINY SEASON

Many people have vacations during the northern summer and so are obliged to hike during the wet season. Don't despair! You can go backpacking at this time and still enjoy yourself; here are some hints.

For day hikes you can start early in the morning, hike all day and return to a dry room at night. Carry your rain gear and if it rains, enjoy the fresh smell, the peeps of sun between the showers, and the rainbows. On longer trips, be patient. Rainy-season mornings are generally dry, so if you rise at dawn you'll still have 6 to 10 hours of dry hiking.

A big problem when backpacking in the wet season is the extremely muddy condition of the trails. Some people insist on using rubber boots or jungle boots, but you might find yourself perfectly happy with ankle-hugging , fabric boots, which are not only lighter, but dry out quicker, and thus give the feet less fungus problems. A little mud on your legs needn't spoil your trip. It is well worth hiking during the wet season. Once you get mentally attuned and used to the rain you'll find many advantages: few other hikers, friendlier villagers and greener countryside. The damp forest scents are unforgettable. Huge, heavy tropical clouds make for spectacular sunsets and sunrises which you can almost touch and smell. Your senses are heightened.

GEAR FOR WET-SEASON HIKING

You don't want to tramp through wet jungles or up rainy mountains sweating profusely in waterproof clothing. There are several solutions. You can buy Gore-Tex rain gear, which allows at least some of your perspiration to escape. You can wear a rain poncho which is loose-fitting enough to prevent much perspiration, or you can wear your rain gear over underwear, or swim suit, instead of clothes, thus keeping your clothes nice and dry inside your pack. If you're sure you won't be exposed to high winds and cold temperatures, you can dispense with rain gear and have one set of wet clothes and one set of dry clothes.

Remember that wool keeps its warmth when wet but cotton doesn't. The same distinction applies between down (useless when wet) and artificial filling such as polarguard or dacron (warm when wet). The best clothing for cold, wet weather is artificial pile. Bring a wool hat and if you get chilly, wear it. Up to 40% of your body heat escapes through your head. Always remember to pack your dry clothes in plastic bags — backpacks are rarely completely waterproof. Finally, if you don't want to be scrambling in and out of rain gear each time it showers, bring a collapsible umbrella! The combination of an umbrella to keep your upper body dry and rain pants to keep your lower body dry works well in all but the most severe rain.

In the heat of the tropics wet clothes mildew very fast, so at the end of a hike, wash and dry your clothes thoroughly.

Your tent must be completely waterproof. New tents are sold without their seams sealed so if your tent didn't come with sealant you'll need to buy some (available at any good camping store) and seal it yourself; otherwise it'll leak like a sieve in the first rainstorm. The same applies to most rain gear. Allow plenty of time for this before you leave on your trip. Or you can try and spend each night in a village or a mountain hut and forget about your tent.

In damp weather using a stove is preferable to trying to light a fire, but if you must have a fire, bring fire-starting ribbon which is available in tubes such as toothpaste comes in. Remember those waterproof matches, or keep ordinary ones dry in a film canister.

Insects can be a problem during the wet season so bring plenty of repellent and apply frequently and thoroughly.

TOPO MAPS AND FINDING YOUR WAY
by Steven Vale

Even with a detailed route description, many hikers like to bring along a topographical map. It adds to the enjoyment of the walk, helps with preliminary planning and enables you to chart your progress and to deviate from the route described. We've tried to give details on where to buy topographical maps throughout Mexico, and to specify the appropriate map for each trail.

In Mexico there are still few up-to-date maps being produced, and those that are seem to be based on satellite photos that are almost 20 years old. In Mexico City maps can be purchased from INEGI (Instituto Nacional de Estadística Geográfica e Informática) at Balderas 71, almost directly opposite the Metro's Juárez Exit, on the Indios Verdes/ Universidad route. Look for the SPP building across the street, to the left. Turn right on entering the building for the sale of maps. Ask to see the *Inventario de Información Geográfica* and you will be given a sheet theoretically showing that maps are available covering the whole country at a scale of 1:50,000. However, every map I asked for was unavailable, though I did manage to get something on Colima National Park and Volcán El Chichonal.

Here follows a list of INEGI's main regional offices:

Paseo Montejo 442, Edificio Oasis, CP 97100, Mérida, Yucatán.

Av. Alcalde 788, casi Esq. Jesús García Sector Hidalgo, CP 44100, Guadalajara, Jalisco.

Felipe Pescador 706 Oriente, entre Laureano Roncal y Voladores, CP 34000 Durango.

Calz. Porfirio Díaz 241, "A" Col. Reforma, CP 68040, Oaxaca.

Independencia 1025, Centro, CP 78000 San Luis Potosí, S.L.P.
Carretera a Bahía Kino Km 0.5, CP 83220 Hermosillo, Son.

Av. Eugenio Garza Sada 1702 Sur, Col. Nuevo Repueblo, CP 64700 Monterrey, N.L.

11 Poniente 1711, Col. San Matias, CP 72000 Puebla, Pue.

Hidalgo Ote. 1227, P.B., Esq. Jaime Nuño, CP 50000 Toluca, Edo. de Mex.

By the time you read this a further source of information may be available for such places as the Monte Azules Biosphere Reserve in the Lacandón and the newly created Triunfo Biosphere Reserve (expected to be a hiker's paradise) in the Sierra Madre del Sur. For addresses see the section on Chiapas.

There is now a US office address for Mexican maps. Write to PO Box 7577, Calexico, CA 92231. Ask for their Inventario de Información Geográfica, which is a list of available maps.

SPANISH

However competent you become with the language there are certain words and phrases that are essential for backpackers and may not be part of your language course.

Words

Footpath — *camino, sendero*
Small village or settlement — *aldea, colonia*
Cornfield or clearing — *milpa*
Farmer or peasant — *campesino*
Backpack — *mochila*
Tent — *carpa*
Motorized canoe or boat — *lancha*

Phrases

No puede perdirse — You can't get lost.
¿Como se llama este lugar? — What's this place called?
¿Qué aldea es esta? — What village is this?
¿Adonde va este camino? — Where does this trail go?
¿De donde viene usted? — Where are you coming from?
¿De donde es usted? — Where are you from (your country)?

The term "gringo" is applied to all light-skinned foreigners and is not usually abusive. Many country people know no other word to use for foreigners.

Chapter 4

On the Road

BUSES

Mexican Buses are a Bargain

Bus service throughout Mexico is fairly good to downright excellent and always a bargain. No worries about getting lost, buying dirty gas, hitting unbarricaded, open manholes in the streets, cows wandering down the road at dusk, or being hit by the local traffic cop hoping to supplement his income... Buses are easier on the pocketbook *and* the nerves.

First-class Mexican buses usually run on time; even rickety buses plying backcountry roads are surprisingly punctual. Maybe even more important than being on time is that most bus drivers, baggage loaders and ticket-takers usually behave in a very professional manner. In Mexico, working for a bus company is regarded as fairly prestigious, and passengers benefit from the workers' pride in what they're doing.

Miscellaneous Bus-Riding Facts

• A first-class ticket from Nuevo Laredo, on the Texas/ Mexico border, to Poza Rica, Veracruz — a 7½-hour trip costs approximately US$12.75.

• In many towns, especially smaller ones, no specific building serves as a bus terminal. *El terminal* may consist of nothing more than a gravel area next to the municipal market, or an unmarked parking area on a street where buses habitually park, load and unload passengers.

• In Mexico distinctions usually are made between first-class and second-class buses, though sometimes the differences are hardly apparent to outsiders. In general, first-class buses cost a little more than second-class ones, are less likely to stop along the road for anyone who flags them down (and thus travel faster), and in them you're more likely to have a seat number assigned, which ensures that you won't be standing. The cost differential between first-class buses and perpetually stopping, wondrously full second-class ones is so small that it's best to go first class if time is a factor, even if you're on a shoestring budget. On the other hand, second-class bus rides often provide memorable and colorful experiences.

• In larger towns, first-class and second-class terminals are frequently in different places. For example, you may arrive at the first-class ADO terminal in Villahermosa, heading for Palenque, only to find that no tickets are available for the rest of the day. Don't despair; just ask where the second-class terminal is, walk a few blocks, and there you'll find a variety of bus lines offering service either all the way to Palenque, or to an intermediate destination, where you can take another bus that will carry you closer.

• Departure times on bus-company schedule-boards are usually noted in the European system. Thus 6am is shown as 600 or 0600, and 6pm is 1800.

• To catch a bus from alongside the road, wave your arm up and down or simply hold your arm at about 11 o'clock, with your hand open. Keep signing for the bus to stop until you're *absolutely sure* the driver intends to do so.

• Many buses, instead of originating at the terminal in which you're buying your ticket, are only passing through — you'll get a ticket on them only if a seat is available. Buses just passing through are said to be traveling *de paso*. If your bus is coming *de paso* and it's first-class, you must wait until it is announced before you can attempt to buy a ticket. If your first-class *de paso* bus is full, as sometimes they are on weekends and holidays, then you just have to wait for another one; on second-class buses they can always squeeze in one more passenger, who will certainly be standing.

• When you pay for your ticket it's possible that you'll be asked to pay a bit more than that posted. If you bring this to the agent's attention, inevitably he'll mention taxes, service charges, or maybe that the posted prices are simply out of date. In view of the crush of humanity desperately trying to get tickets and the probability that you'll have to pay the higher price anyway, unless the price is outrageously higher, it's usually just best to let it slide.

• The ticket agent may write your bus's number on your ticket. Else he may provide the gate number or bay number in which the bus is parked. And it's quite possible that the agent won't know any of this information, and you'll just have to figure it out for yourself.

• When your ticket is handed over, confirm that the date (*fecha*) and time (*hora*) are correct. The price you paid is the *valor*, and your seat number is given in the box marked *asiento*.

• When you find your bus, if you have a backpack, instead of getting into line to enter the bus, go stand beside the baggage bay. Eventually the attendant should tag your equipment and give you a baggage check. Don't worry about others getting on the bus before you; if you have a seat number, you're guaranteed a seat. On second-class buses, having to wait outside to store baggage certainly is a problem unless you have a friend who can enter before you, and claim two seats.

• Inside the bus, seat numbers usually appear in little windows on the side of the baggage rack over the passengers' heads. The windows may say something like "VENT 18 PAS 19." This means that the window seat is #18 (VEN for *ventana* means "window"), and the aisle seat is #19 (PAS for *pasillo* means "aisle"). If you were issued no seat number, you can sit (or stand) wherever you wish.

• Bus trips in Mexico are fairly informal, laid-back affairs; during the trip, *groove* with the bus driver's mariachi music being played on the tape-deck mounted above the windshield next to the decal of the Virgin of Guadalupe and beneath the red-bangled curtain, and when vendors at intermediate stops stream onto the bus or gather outside windows selling not only *refrescos*, but also plastic bags of peeled oranges, roasted peanuts, hot tamales wrapped in corn shucks, local sweetbreads... *enjoy* (taking precautions with regard to diarrhea)!

• Here are some phrases that come in handy when buying bus tickets:

"*Un boleto para el autobús que sale a las nueve para Amecameca, por favor.* "A ticket for the bus that leaves at 9:00 for Amecameca, please."

"*Qué es el número de mi autobús?*" "What's my bus's number?"

"*¿Es este el autobús que sale a las nueve para Amecameca?*" "Is this the bus that leaves for Amecameca at nine o'clock?"

"*Si usted oye el anuncio para Amecameca, ¿puede usted avisarme?*" "If you hear the announcement for Amecameca, will you please let me know?"

"*¿Sabe usted cual autobús va a Amecameca?*" "Do you know which bus goes to Amecameca?"

"*¿Ya ha llegado el autobús para Amecameca?*" — "Has the bus for Amecameca arrived yet?"

TRAINS

by Steven Vale

Travel by train is slow though the exceptional scenery helps make up for it. The justly famous Los Mochis to Chihuahua run (see the section on Copper Canyon) is one of the world's great train rides. Fast, modern trains are supposed to run between the border town of Mexicali and Mexico City, and others are supposed to serve Monterrey, Guadalajara, Veracruz and Mérida, but in reality these are often delayed and can be painfully slow. Ordinary first class offers air-conditioned compartments for approximately the same price as a first-class bus journey. *Primera Especial* offers wide, airline-style seats, which recline slightly, have ample leg-room, air-conditioning and airline-style meals; this ticket costs twice as much as ordinary first class. Standards vary enormously. My first trip, a night journey, was in a spotlessly clean compartment and we were served a reasonable meal. However, on a day-long trip between Guadalajara and Mazatlán our *Primera Especial* compartment was as dilapidated as second class. The toilet was vile, the carpet filthy, our window consisted of a broken blind covering shattered glass, and the air-conditioning ceased operation with 6 hours of the journey remaining.

LODGING

There are, of course, all classes of hotel and restaurants throughout Mexico. If you're not on a tight budget you'll find that many of the hotels, *posadas, quintas* and *albergues* are charming, of good value, and much more enjoyable than the international hotel chains.

At a cheaper level are the *hospedajes* and *pensiones*, which in many places can be found for US$5.00 or less. These rock bottom places are extremely basic: no hot water, no hygiene, lumpy and sometimes flea-infested beds, a large variety of the local fauna scurrying about the floor and up the walls — but with loads of atmosphere.

FOOD

Don't forget Dr. Bob's warning in the diarrhea section: *Boil it, cook it, peel it or forget it!* Well, this warning, in a sense, is as much an invitation to eat well and cheaply as it is to stay on guard and to eat in more expensive places with fancy menus.

LOCAL DISHES

With such a distinctive cuisine you may need a little help with what to eat in Mexico. Here are some ideas:

Mole   A chocolate-based sauce containing chile and sometimes coconut.

Mole poblana   Turkey and *mole* with almonds.

Chile relleno   Batter-covered green pepper filled with cheese or meat.

Tamales   Stuffed cornmeal "envelopes" steamed in a corn husk or banana leaf.

Enchilada   Stuffed tortilla (thin corn pancakes) often served with a rich sauce or sour cream.

Torta   A type of sandwich (not cake as in some other countries).

Huevos rancheros   Eggs with hot sauce.

Guacamole   Avocado mashed with onions and various seasonings.

Cecina enchilada   Fried slivers of beef with a spicy coating (Oaxaca).

This is because when we're at the very kind of place where the cheapest Mexican soul-food is available, the *comedor*, you can watch your food being prepared in front of you, and you can make sure that what you get is hot enough (temperature-hot) to deactivate the most insidious bacteria.

Most *comedores* are open-walled stalls set up along streets near bus stations, in *mercados*, or just anyplace where people get hungry. Usually there's a single *señora* with a stove or an open fire; you sit down, say what you want, and you watch the whole process from egg-shell cracking to consumption. The fare isn't fancy at all; often you're not even given a fork, and must deftly use a tortilla as a scoop. Usually they offer some kind of meat stew (which you must avoid unless it's boiling hot), beans, rice, tortillas and eggs — that's about it, and often the *señora* must take your money in advance and go buy the eggs. To order "Mexican eggs" (scrambled, with bits of onion, tomato and chili), with black beans and rice, and coffee, (tortillas come automatically) say, "*Una porción, por favor, de huevos a la mejicana, frijoles y arróz, y una taza de café*. If you can't appreciate the joys of chili, to say "without chili," add *sin chili*. Of course, one key to eating in *comedores* without getting diarrhea is to choose the ones that look clean and well organized. If food looks cold or sits in open pots, or if the *señora*'s apron is really foul-looking, forget it. Always ask the cost of a dish before ordering it.

Hilary Bradt says that the only truly bad case of diarrhea she's ever contracted was from an upscale, expensive restaurant. That's often the case. You shouldn't depend on food handlers working behind closed doors to keep in mind your delicate *gringo* sensitivities.

With regard to ordering in a land where you don't know the names of all the foods, don't hesitate to point at things on the plates of other customers. It works, and Mexicans have such great senses of humor that they don't think it's at all gauche.

MONEY

The Mexican peso is written as $, which may give you a shock the first time you see the price of something. There are 100 centavos to the peso and in 1992 you got about 3,000 pesos for one U.S. dollar. There is no black market worth mentioning. VISA credit cards can be used to obtain cash advances at some banks.

MEXICO CITY

Many travellers will start their trip by flying to Mexico City. The capital is very large, very noisy and very polluted. Many travelers try to stay out of it, but it does have a lot to offer culturally and architecturally. Even if you're normally a museum hater, do visit the Museum of Anthropology. The building and the exhibits are rightly world famous. Don't miss the ethnological displays (upstairs) which are of great interest to backpackers who may be hiking among some of the Indian tribes.

Cheapish accommodation can be found around the Monument to the Revolution west of the Alemeda. Reasonable hotels here include the **Hotel Oxford, Gran Hotel Texas** and **Hotel Carlton**; expect to pay between US$10 to US$15 for a double room.

The tourist office, at Calle Masarik 172, Colonia Polanco, is open from 8am to 1pm. Best to buy a map from a bookshop as soon as you arrive, though, or in advance from Bradt Publications (*Mexico City Tourist Map*).

City Transport

In Mexico City the Metro is fast, cheap and efficient. Sometimes the police won't allow backpacks to be carried on it but if you go during "off hours," such as 10:30am, 2pm, or during the nights, usually you can get by with it. City buses are equally efficient, though wrestling with a backpack inside a bus is awkward. Long-distance buses depart from four different terminals in Mexico City, so if you're coming from California and planning to continue on to Chiapas, for instance, you must cross town; that's when you become thankful for the metros, because for pennies they'll whisk you from one to the other, faster than any taxi.

The four terminals and the names of their Metro stops are, for the north, **Terminal Autobuses del Norte**; east, **San Lázaro**; south, **Taxqueña**, and; west, **Observatorio**. Note that service to Chiapas is provided at the eastern terminal, not the southern one. The Metro stop within easy walking distance of the international airport is **Terminal Aérea** on the Politecnico/ Pantitlán Line, *not* the one called Aeropuerto.

Chapter 5

Natural History

THE LAND ITSELF

Mexico north of the Isthmus of Tehuantepec — all of the country except Baja, the Yucatán Peninsula and Chiapas — is shaped like a horn-of-plenty, with the southern base curved toward the east. In the middle of this horn there's a highland that's something like a V-shaped, high-elevation bowl. This bowl, which is an arid, deserty one, has its eastern rim formed by the Eastern Sierra Madre Mountains; the Western Sierra Madres form its western rim. Both of the pine-clad Sierra Madre chains provide fine hiking almost anyplace you can gain access to them, and quite a few highways do cross them. In general, the farther south you travel inside the high-elevation bowl, the higher in elevation you'll rise. Just south of Mexico City a band of volcanos — some of them still active — runs east and west. On the highland's eastern side there's a strip of hot, humid land called the Gulf lowlands; on the western side, the Pacific lowlands also are hot and humid.

Jutting south below the U.S. state of California, Mexican Baja California is a world unto itself. It also has Pacific lowlands and Gulf lowlands, though here it's the Gulf of California, not the Gulf of Mexico. You'll see that in our Baja section Graham Mackintosh says that you can circumnavigate the entire peninsula, walking along the coast. A mountain range forms Baja's geographical spine. The uplands are served with a network of trails — often the remnants of historic trails uniting colonial missions. Add the fact that Baja's plants and animals are uncommonly interesting and unique, and you have to say that Baja is as much a hiker's dreamland as is mainland Mexico.

The Yucatán Peninsula, with rainforests in the south evolving into arid thorn-forests in the north, is a huge, flat to gently rolling, low-elevation slab of limestone. Some very interesting hiking can be made visiting ancient, out-of-the-way Maya ruins.

That leaves Chiapas, Mexico's southernmost state, adjoining Guatemala. Chiapas's plants and animals show more affinities with Central America than they do with the rest of Mexico, and the diversity of life forms here is greater than anywhere else in Mexico. Chiapas is home to the most traditional of Mexico's indigenous peoples, thus requiring special sensitivity and watchfulness on the hiker's part. Its Lacandón Jungle and isolated peaks provide some of the most exotic feelings available in Mexico.

VEGETATION ZONES

In very general terms, all other things being equal, as you travel south in Mexico annual rainfall increases and vegetation becomes more lush: deserts in the north, rainforest in the south.

The north's arid zone, however, is far from being one unified desert. In one place you may see horizon to horizon mesquite, but eventually this gives way to horizon to horizon rocky soil populated with towering saguaro cacti or Joshua trees, or maybe there'll be grasslands or brushy chaparral — and each vegetation type has its own particular assemblage of animals. Where mountains rise up, vegetation patterns become even more diverse. In the Baja section you'll see how to walk across the desert and climb up to an oak/pine forest — an ecological island high in the clouds.

Sometimes rainfall on one side of a mountain will be extremely heavy and the vegetation will be very lush, but on the other side, in the "rain shadow", there will be nothing but cacti and a few clumps of grass. Vegetation on mountain slopes usually occurs in fairly predictable zones. At the base of mountains in hot, humid areas you might find dense, exceedingly humid and lush rainforest; above this zone, tropical deciduous forest may develop, whose trees are smaller than those in a rainforest, and may lose their leaves, especially during the dry season; next come the slope oak/pine forest appears, with oak coming first, giving way to pine as elevation increases, until finally there may be nothing but pine; eventually spruce and fir appear, and above that, instead of trees, you'll find alpine meadows and snowfields.

SOME ANIMALS YOU MIGHT MEET

Nine-Banded Armadillo

These endearing animals are quite common, and you'll often see them shuffling around in leaves or grass, hunting out insects and other small creatures, then digging frantically to reach their meal. With their noses so often buried deep in the ground, it's convenient that armadillos can hold their breath for up to six minutes. They have poor hearing and even poorer eyesight but an excellent sense of smell.

Coati or Coatimundi

You're unlikely to travel far in back-country Mexico without meeting a coati, either in the wild or as a pet. They are playful and affectionate pets, but their long, whiffly noses get into everything and they are very destructive. Coatis belong to the same family as raccoons, and live in tropical forests where they are particularly active in the early morning and evening, foraging in troops of up to thirty, although they may also be solitary, in which case they are called coatimundis. They are excellent tree climbers and may, at first glance, be mistaken for monkeys as they shinny up trees in search of fruit or tasty insects.

Collared Peccary

Peccaries are species of wild pig living in a variety of habitats throughout Mexico. They are highly gregarious and you sometimes see groups of them; because they've been overhunted, it's more likely you'll see their hoofprints, especially around watering holes. Peccaries secrete musk so you often smell them before you see them. Adults can be aggressive and are capable of inflicting serious wounds with their sharp tusks. A woodsman in Chiapas told Jim Conrad that of all the animals in the Lacandón forest he feared this animal most because, he said, "it's so stupid". If you surprise one on a trail, it may try to escape by running right over you, slashing with its tusks, instead of running away.

Howler Monkey

Howlers, in Mexico found mostly in Chiapas's Lacandón Jungle and the southern Yucatán Peninsula, are usually heard before they're seen. If you camp at Maya Bell Campground near Palenque, you might hear them each morning; more than howl, they roar — like a lion. You won't soon forget it if you're hiking down the trail to Bonampak and a howler unexpectedly lets it rip from not far away. Howler monkeys move around in troops, and the troop leader is responsible for the dawn and dusk howling concerts, although others join in. The male has a huge voice box, strengthened with cartilage, which enables him to project the sound so impressively. Being the largest of the American monkeys also helps.

Spider Monkey

Though spider monkeys have no thumbs their bodies are beautifully adapted to tree life; they are the most efficient climbers and swingers of all the New World monkeys. It's a joy to watch them moving effortlessly through the trees, making prodigious leaps, and using their tails as hands. In fact the tail has a hairless area on the underside which can feel as efficiently as a finger, so the tail really is a fifth limb. You'll always be able to distinguish spider monkeys from howlers because the spiders have such long limbs.

Birds

Europe has a little over 500 bird species, North America north of Mexico has in the vicinity of 650, and in Mexico itself you can see more than 1000. Obviously it's impossible here to provide more than a peep at Mexico's more colorful and interesting birds.

First, the river birds. Since river travel is leisurely and comfortable, there is ample opportunity for birdwatching and you will see far more species than during a walk in the jungle when they're all out of sight in the treetops, and your pack makes it difficult to look above you anyway. Any marshy area is full of jacanas, also known as lily-trotters; they're the ones with long, long toes and yellow wings visible only when they fly. Anhingas or snake-birds — gawky black birds with white wing patches and long necks — are common down some rivers. Their long, snaky neck is often the only part visible above the water's surface, but you're more likely to see them standing motionless in the sun drying their wings. Herons and egrets need no introduction and the various kingfishers are easily recognizable.

Moving on to tropical forest, this is the habitat of a huge variety of birds, but you will need binoculars to spot them in the concealing foliage. Parrots can be easily recognized. You are much more likely to see them as they fly home in the evening than in the trees where they noisily prepare for the night. Parrots usually fly in pairs, although larger flocks are also common; you can recognize them by their rapid wingbeats and their habit of squawking at one another as they fly. Mexican parrots are basically green with other colors on their heads and wings.

Toucans favor humid tropical forests, while their smaller cousins the toucanets prefer cloud forests. Toucanets have a more slender bill than the true toucan, but are still distinctive, especially in silhouette. Trogons are widely distributed, although the most famous of the family, the quetzal, lives only in certain cloud forests. In Mexico it has been hunted to the verge of extinction. All trogons have the same bright green plumage and red or yellow breasts, but only the male quetzal has a golden sheen to its green feathers and magnificent tail.

Happily, there's an excellent field guide to Mexican birds. It's *A Field Guide to Mexican Birds* by Roger Tory Peterson and Edward L. Chalif; 1973, Houghton and Mifflin, Boston. Note that this guide only illustrates species not found farther north; the well equipped birder in Mexico must carry both the Mexican guide, and a guide to U.S. and Canadian birds.

PEOPLE IN THE LANDSCAPE

Along the Trail

One of the delights of hiking most of the trails profiled in this book is that on the trails you come into contact with many varied faces of Mexican society. You walk through pastures full of cows, pass under trees heavy with avocados or papayas, brush by coffee bushes, and stroll past beach huts where fishermen set out their day's catch to dry.

Women run shyly past you on their way to market, men straighten from their stooping position to greet you before continuing to work their *milpas* (cornfields), gangs of children shout questions as they trudge to school, and old grannies stop for a chat. Domestic animals are everywhere; pigs snuffle and root in the undergrowth, brahma calves flick their lop-ears at your passing, and hysterical dogs burst from their huts at your arrival.

Conservation

In the earliest incarnation of this guide, which appeared in 1982, some remarks by Dennis Glick, then of the Wildlands Management Unit, Centro Agronómico Tropical de Investigación y Ensenanza (CATIE), of Costa Rica, were included. Though his remarks were mainly with regard to conditions in Central America, today they are just as appropriate for Mexico. Therefore, we're including them again.

He spoke of an "environmental crisis which is rapidly converting many regions of Central America into wastelands. Costa Rica for example, loses some 60,000ha (150,000 acres) of forests yearly; a third of Guatemala's Petén has been deforested in the last 10 years; 100% of all sea turtle eggs deposited on the Pacific coast of Honduras are collected and sold as *bocas*; cotton farmers in Nicaragua and El Salvador apply U.S.-banned agrochemicals 15-30 times a year on their fields, etc., etc. With a population that is expected to double within the next 25 years these problems will certainly become even more severe. Any forest that is not protected within the boundaries of a national park or equivalent reserve will surely be gone by the end of the century."

As foreign visitors we may feel helpless and unable to participate in conservation efforts in this part of the world, but Dennis points out that "If foreign visitors are going to derive recreational pleasures from these Central American wildlands they should conversely become actively involved in their protection. Both governmental and nongovernmental conservation related interests in developing countries should be pressured by these people to become more committed to promoting or supporting wildland management projects in the Mesoamerican region. We don't need visitors that are merely 'recreational imperialists,' i.e. taking but not giving anything in return."

Perhaps salvation for Mexico's wildlands lies in developing its national parks to be really attractive for tourists, and making wildlife-watching big business, as in East Africa. Whatever the answer, if you, the visitor, see and enjoy Mexico's natural wonders, please the country's decision-makers by spending some money in out-of-the-way places, and add your voice to those supporting environmental protection. It can only help.

NOTE The following organizations are actively involved in conservation in Mexico and all publish newsletters or other interesting pamphlets:

Ducks Unlimited, One Waterfowl Way at Gilmer Rd., Long Grove, IL 60014
Nature Conservancy, 1815 N. Lynn St., Arlington, VA 22209.
World Wildlife Fund, 1250 24th St. NW, Washington DC 20037.
Worldwatch Institute, 1776 Massachusetts Ave. N.W., Washington, D.C. 20036, U.S.A.
International Union for the Conservation of Nature and Natural Resources (IUCN), I I 10 Morges, Switzerland.
PRONATUR, Avenida Nuevo León No. 144, Col. Hipodromo Condesa, 06100 Mexico, D.F.

Visiting Isolated Villages

No hiker wants to have a negative impact on the isolated communities he or she visits. Therefore, we must always try to reduce our impact on the people whose villages we pass through.

Of course we can remain somewhat aloof, camping between villages and avoiding contact with local people. This is the least disturbing to them, but perhaps the least satisfying for the traveler. Or we can spend time in villages, getting to know the locals as individuals, sharing food and shelter, exchanging life histories, and generally becoming involved. This is, of course, the most rewarding if the hiker has a good knowledge of Spanish and is a friendly, warm and open person.

If this is the way you expect to travel, you should be well prepared. For instance, remember that hospitality is a time-honored custom in any isolated community, and a stranger will almost always be offered food and shelter. This does not mean there is food enough for everyone, and although one visitor will make little impact, a couple or more will, and should reciprocate with their own gifts of food. Chocolate always is good to carry; it's not an alien food (chocolate was "invented" by indigenous Mexicans), is enjoyed by all but is seldom available. We've also given away packets of soup, granola bars and cans of sardines, but with some hesitation, not wanting to help develop a taste for the exotic. Other welcome presents are nylon twine, matches, candles, and so on; color pictures of our families and postcards of home can be the source of endless conversations and stories. Other useless but fun things such as a frisbee, or a loop of string and an infinite knowledge of cat's cradles, or a piece of paper and skill in the art of origami can elevate a hiker to the role of super-*gringo* without disturbing that native culture one jot.

Indian markets and fiestas

In all countries with an indigenous population markets and festivals play a prominent part in village live.

Weekly or daily markets are held in almost every town and village throughout Mexico and it is here that each town displays its individuality. One morning in a market will teach you a great deal about the place; the produce grown in the area, the traditional costumes worn by the women (and some men) and the town's facilities. Although Ladino markets sell useful or tasty goods, it's the Indian village markets that attract tourists. For the inhabitants it's the most important day of the week and they make the best of it, walking in from neighboring areas carrying the goods they wish to sell, and walking unsteadily out again (men, that is) after some cheerful hours of drinking with their friends. The women enjoy their traditional pursuit of gossiping as they sit beside their little pyramids of tomatoes, lemons, tangerines, and so on. Everything is conducted quietly; no voices are raised except for those of tourists striking a bargain. There is no striving to sell, and indeed I've heard a story of an Indian woman refusing to sell her last few lemons because then she would have to go home and it was still early.

If you go to markets to buy Indian handicrafts you will be expected to bargain. There is no rule as to what percentage of the first price quoted you can expect to pay. Don't be rude with your bargaining and denigrate the product. This is not the Indian way. Much better to praise it but regret your lack of money.

While markets are a quiet hum of activity, fiestas explode with sound. There is music and dancing, and often a display of fireworks in the evening. "Banger" rockets are let off all day in a nerve-shattering way, particularly in villages with a lot of ladinos, who always love noise.

Indian fiestas are often a fascinating blend of Christianity and paganism. Fiestas are held on religious and patriotic holidays, but it is only the religious ones that are of interest to tourists. In Mexico there are national fiestas such as Holy Week and All Souls' Days, and village fiestas when the patron saint is honored. Go to any village named after the saint whose day it is and you'll find a fiesta. Both national and local festivals are fascinating, but a small village fiesta is probably the most delightful, with all the local people dressing up to the nines.

Ritual drunkenness is another cheerful hangover from earlier days. After a few days of fiesta you can see long-suffering wives and daughters bearing their tipsy men-folk home. There are lots of pre-conquest features in modern fiestas. Dances, for instance, often symbolize the Four Cardinal Points sacred to the Maya, and you'll often see mirrors, either in the costumes of dancers or in the decorative arches above the church door, which symbolize the warrior god Tezcatlipoca of the Smoking Mirror.

SOME FIESTA DAYS IN MEXICO

January 20	Day of San Sebastián
March 19	Day of San José
April 25	Day of San Marcos
June 13	Day of San Antonio
June 24	Day of San Juan
June 29	Day of San Pedro and San Pablo
July 25	Day of Santiago
July 30	Day of San Cristóbal
August 4	Day of Santo Domingo
October 4	Day of San Francisco
November 1-2	All Saints' and All Souls' Days
November 11	Day of San Martín
November 25	Day of Santa Catarina
November 30	Dan of San Andrés
December 4	Day of Santa Barbara
December 16-24	Posada season
December 25	Christmas Day
December 28	All Fools' Day

Movable:	
Carnival	The week before Ash Wednesday
Palm Sunday	The Sunday before Easter
Holy Week	All Easter week but mainly Thursday and Friday

| Holy Saturday | Day before Easter Day |
| Easter Day | Religious services rather than fiesta |

Note: Fiestas are often held on the Sunday nearest the saint's day.

Part Two

The Hikes

THE GLOBETROTTERS CLUB

An international club which aims to share information on adventurous budget travel through monthly meetings and *Globe* magazine. Published every two months, *Globe* offers a wealth of information from reports of members' latest adventures to travel bargains and tips, plus the invaluable 'Mutual Aid' column where members can swap a house, sell a camper, find a travel companion or offer information on unusual places or hospitality to visiting members. London meetings are held monthly (Saturdays) and focus on a particular country or continent with illustrated talks.

Enquiries to: Globetrotters Club, BCM/Roving, London WC1N 3XX.

Chapter 6

Baja California

by Graham Mackintosh

GENERAL INFORMATION

Baja is almost 1300km (800mi) long and generally less than 130km (80mi) wide. Its two coasts are very different from one another. The Pacific coast has a churning surf and mornings can be cool and misty; the eastern coast, on the Gulf of California, is more tranquil and hotter; in the summer the Gulf coast's temperatures generally are 8 to 11°C (15 to 20°F) hotter than beaches at the same latitude on the Pacific side.

A mountainous backbone runs the peninsula's length. Moving inland from the sun-baked and arid coast, one finds unexpected palm canyons flowing with spring water and, at the highest elevations, "islands" of pine forests with lakes. The tallest peak, Picacho del Diablo, is 3,087m (10,126ft) high, and often covered with snow in the winter.

Baja's northeastern corner is the hottest and most desolate. Otherwise, as one approaches the U.S. border the desert gives way to chaparral, coniferous forest and coastal sage scrub. At Baja's southern tip, below La Paz, increased rainfall increases the vegetation's lushness.

From mainland Mexico ferry services operate from Guaymas to Santa Rosalía, and from Topolobampo and Mazatlán to La Paz. From the U.S. there are regular flights to Tijuana, Loreto, La Paz and Los Cabos. By road from the U.S. there are five official border crossings — at Tijuana, Otay Mesa, Tecate, Mexicali and Algodones. Most visitors cross at Tijuana and pick up the toll road to Ensenada before following Hwy 1 down the peninsula. Buses run the length of the peninsula and most of the major highways.

Regular customs regulations are in effect in Baja, except that no auto permit is required. U.S. dollars are accepted everywhere. Baja's cost of living — especially at hotels and restaurants — is generally higher than in the rest of Mexico, but one can camp almost anywhere for free.

COASTAL HIKES
(Hikes listed in order beginning near the US border on the Pacific Side, then counterclockwise around the peninsula)

Background Notes
It's possible to hike Baja's entire coast, from Ensenada to San Felipe, covering an estimated 4,800km (3,000mi), hardly ever encountering a manmade barrier. On the coast, your equipment, planning and determination — not geography — set the limits on how far you go and how long you stay.

La Bufadora

Orientation
Across the bay from Ensenada, La Bufadora is a collection of tourist houses and trailers, restaurants, food stands and curio shops built around what's reputed to be the biggest blow-hole in the world — a place where waves rush into a nearly submerged cave, air inside the cave compresses, and air and water explode in a booming spout of foam and spray high into the air. The blow-hole itself is called La Bufadora, which means "the blower" ("the snorter").

Vegetation in this area is coastal scrub, with plenty of cacti, mainly of the pricklypear kind, and agave. The cactus spines are vicious. Also beware of the surf; several people have been swept off the rocks and drowned. Sunsets can be magnificent, and between December and March it's a great place to watch the annual coastal migration of California gray whales as they journey to and from their breeding and calving grounds in Baja's Pacific Coast lagoons.

Getting There
At Maneadero about 18km (11mi) south of Ensenada, turn right (if you're heading south) from Hwy 1 onto the more-or-less paved road sometimes known as Hwy 23; La Bufadora lies almost at the tip of the rugged Punta Banda Peninsula, which forms the southern limit

of Todos Santos Bay. The road runs about 23km (14mi) to the blow hole. Several places are available for camping; probably you'll have to pay. Trails are numerous.

Camalú to El Rosario

Several easy points of access to the Pacific are available on Hwy 1, especially at Camalú and the entire stretch from San Quintín to El Rosario. At El Rosario Hwy 1 shoots inland; south of El Rosario hundreds of miles of magnificently empty coastline — all the way to Guerrero Negro — provide splendid solitude likely to be interrupted only by few fishcamps and adventurous offroading *gringos*. The truly characteristic Baja desert with its cardón (large, columnar cactus-like plants) and cirios begin at El Rosario.

Santa Rosalillita

About 25 km (15mi) south of Punta Prieta, take the wide, gravel, sign-posted turnoff west to this small fishing village about 16km (10mi) down the road. There are no tourist facilities at Santa Rosalillita, but it's an easy drive (or hitch) in or out.

Running south from Santa Rosalillita a rough road follows the coast for about 25km (15mi). The coast is generally low-lying, offering good beach camping, surfing, shelling and clamming. After a roadless stretch you'll find a road reaching the coast at El Tomatal; then the beach becomes increasingly wide and sandy, and backed by low, rolling dunes. Approaching the rocky headland of Morro Santo Domingo, tree trunks, whale bones and other curiosities begin littering the shore; here you are entering the vast hook of Bahía Sebastián Vizcaíno, also known as Vizcaíno Bay, and comprising some of the world's finest beachcombing.

North of Santa Rosalillita the coast becomes rockier but more beautiful. The thriving sealion colony on Isla Adelaida is worth a visit if you can persuade one of the fishermen to take you there. Farther north Punta Rocosa is a tricky but dramatic stretch of low cliffs and tiny islets. North of that you have a hundred miles of beaches, headlands and fishcamps before reaching El Rosario. A little-used coastal road comes and goes, providing an alternative to the joys and tribulations of coast-walking. You are in the right area for lobsters, clams, abalone and long, empty beaches. If you're not going all the way to El Rosario, keep in mind that you must eventually return to the highway. In the summer don't try to walk out by using any of the roads or trails — it's better to reach a fishcamp and wait for a ride. When the heat is really bad, it can be dangerous heading inland, away from the cooling breezes of the Pacific.

Cedros Island

Cedros Island is the big island west of Bahía Vizcaíno, mid way down the Pacific Coast. The island itself is about 32km (20mi) long and has a population of about 10,000, most of whom live in the town of Cedros on the island's southeastern coast. While not many tourists visit Cedros, there's an airport, bars, restaurants, taxis and inexpensive guest houses. Among the attractions are some fine beaches, sealion colonies and, on the mountains that rise to 1,200m (4,000ft), forests of pine and juniper.

The easiest way to get to Cedros is to fly from Ensenada; Ensenada's airport lies about 8km (5mi) south of town on Hwy 1. There are two roundtrip flights a week, on DC3's. Flying time is a little less than two hours and a oneway ticket costs US$65; once on the island, a US$5 taxi ride carries you to town.

With regard to visiting other islands, it's sometimes possible to hire a fisherman to ferry you anyplace you want to go. Just remember the water problem, and that you should never rely on a friendly fisherman's assurance that he'll be back *mañana*. If his boat breaks down or a storm blows up, you can find yourself marooned on a desert island contemplating the fact that in the summer, without water, your life expectancy is about 24 hours!

Whale-Watching at Laguna San Ignacio

January through March is whale-watching time at Laguna San Ignacio. During my first encounter with the gray whale, I was in a small Mexican fishing boat with five other tourists. Several whales had glided beneath us before one approached and gently nudged the boat. The barnacle-covered creature then raised its head vertically from the water and looked us over. Satisfied with what it saw, it approached the boat over and over again allowing us to reach out and touch its surprisingly soft flesh. That was the pattern for three days — curious mothers and babies, and "friendlies" galore. These gentle creatures couldn't get enough of us, nor we of them.

Local fishermen act as guides when the whales are in the lagoon. Whale-watching costs about US$25 per person per day if you can find an authorized Mexican with room to take you out. Otherwise organized tours are much more expensive. **Baja Discovery** operates a fly-in whale-camp near the lagoon's mouth; in the U.S. phone (800) 829-2252 or (619) 262-0700.

The oasis town of San Ignacio is in the middle of the peninsula, just a mile off Hwy 1, buried in a jungle of date palms planted by Jesuit missionaries. A 50km (30mi) road connects the town of San Ignacio with the bay of San Ignacio.

Baja's Old Mission Trail

by Graham Mackintosh

Though Spanish conquistadors arrived in Baja in 1535, the land was so inhospitable that Baja's first permanent settlement didn't appear until 1697. In that year Jesuit missionaries established a mission at Loreto — the first of a chain of 23, which eventually were connected by a network of trails, much of which still exists.

When the Mexican government secularized the missions in 1832, the land was largely transferred to the Spanish soldiers who had served as guards at the missions. The guards' descendants established isolated ranches on their holdings, and to this day the frontier lifestyle and cowboy traditions of those first settlers live on in their descendants.

The Coast near Todos Santos

Toward the tip of the peninsula, on Hwy 19, Todos Santos makes a good jumping-off point for some great Pacific hiking. South of town, beaches and rocky headlands stretch all the way to Cabo San Lucas; north of town the beaches seem to go on forever. However, this is an area of dangerous currents; the surf tends to dump right on the beach, which often makes it hard to exit the water. On the other hand, from the shore you can cast into deep water and catch big fish.

Between Loreto and Mulegé

Though this is a touristy stretch, it still offers spectacular backpacking. For about 40km (25mi) Hwy 1 parallels Bahía Concepción, offering many beautiful camping beaches. Expect to pay a few dollars and bring insect repellent for the no-seeums. The bay is popular with kayakers and windsurfers. For information on kayaking, snorkeling or clamming day-trips, or to hire kayaks or canoes for longer excursions, contact Roy and Becky at Palapa #17, Playa Santispac, or write them at **Baja Tropicales**, Box 60, Mulegé, B.C.S., Mexico. The Mulegé area is rich in Indian cave painting and petroglyph sites. At km 109, opposite Playa El Burro, there is a steep gully with dozens of petroglyphs. Inland from Mulegé, at La Trinidad, there's a site with important cave paintings. Enquire at Hotel Baja Hacienda, Las Casitas or any Mulegé hotel for information on day trips.

Bahía de Los Ángeles

This beautiful, island-studded bay lies 68km (42mi) from Hwy 1 along a paved road. No buses serve the bay; you must either drive or hitch in; don't expect more than one or two vehicles an hour. As you approach "the Bay of L.A.," you're treated with a great vista — one of the most memorable in Baja. Leave the hotels, restaurants and trailer parks of town and you soon run into wild and wonderful country. The cacti forests here are some of the tallest and most spectacular in the world. Don't try anything too ambitious if you're heading north, for beyond the bay you encounter a long, desolate, dangerous stretch where you may not see anyone for 130km (80mi) or more. Summer temperatures, even near the water, can be 43°C (110°F). The coast is equally rugged to the south, but there is a road running behind the mountains occasionally meeting the shore at places like Bahía de las Ánimas and Bahía San Rafael. Don't expect to see much traffic.

The Coast South of Puertecitos

Tides in the northern Gulf are enormous — up to 9m (30ft)! Keep that in mind when you pitch your tent. Puertecitos is accessible by a more-or-less paved road running south from San Felipe. North of Puertecitos there are too many beachside tourist homes for the coast to be attractive, but south of Puertecitos the coast is more pristine. Although it is often rocky and rugged, one can readily hike inland, and pick up a dirt road that enables you to bypass anything you don't like the look of. While the desert here is comparatively barren and uninteresting, there are some fine beaches for camping, and the many nearby islands are particularly photogenic.

INLAND HIKES

(Listed from north to south)

Background Notes

During Colonial times a system of trails interconnected Baja's numerous missions. Some of these trails evolved into the paved highways we travel today, but others were largely forgotten, abandoned, and left for us to explore. Much of the mileage logged on the following inland walks takes place on old mission trails.

Sierra San Pedro Mártir National Park

Towering over this highland landscape of pine forests, meadows, granite boulders and streams is Baja's tallest peak — 3,087m (10,126ft) Picacho del Diablo. Also in the park, on an east-facing ridge at 2,804m (9,200ft) the 2.13m reflecting telescope of the Mexican National Observatory takes advantage of the area's crystal-clear air. May to August is the best time to visit; snow can close the road in winter. Even midsummer nights can seem freezing at this altitude, so bring something warm.

The best route to the park is by taking the bone-shaking washboard-road leading off Hwy 1 about 130km (80mi) south of Ensenada. You'll pass through San Telmo village and Meling Ranch, a working cattle ranch with a spring-fed swimming pool which offers accommodation and horse and mule trips into the high country. Beyond the ranch you pass through chaparral and eventually reach the treeline and the park entrance. A small fee may be charged if there's anyone at the gate to take your money. Once inside, you'll feel as if you have a whole biological island to yourself, with its native trout and 19 species of endemic plants. Another 79 plant species found here are encountered nowhere else in Baja.

Cataviña and Beyond

Midway between El Rosario and Guerrero Negro, Cataviña is an incredible natural rock garden where cirios and cardóns rise from wind-sculptured, granite boulders. Rare blue fanpalms line the arroyos, which sometimes flow with water. A mile or so south of the La Pinta Hotel, there are very reasonably priced meals and accommodations at **Rancho Santa Inés**; for a small fee you can camp and use the showers. From Santa Inés, a rarely used and probably undriveable road runs 23km (14mi) east to an oasis and the ruins of the old Jesuit mission of Santa María de los Ángeles. You can make that the goal of your hike, or join the Mission Trail there.

San Francisco de la Sierra

San Francisco de la Sierra is worth visiting because of the area's extremely impressive cave paintings; the best require a day's hike or a mule ride. To reach San Francisco take the signposted road at Km 118, 45km (28mi) northwest of San Ignacio. At first the road is broad and easy, but soon it deteriorates as it climbs 37km (23mi) into the mountains. A high-clearance vehicle is recommended.

Arriving at the village, to visit the cave paintings, it's the law that you must "sign in" and hire a guide, which costs about US$20 per day. Mules and burros are available for about US$25 per animal per day, and you are expected to feed your guide. The descent to the canyon bottom is spectacular, and the paintings are more so. After a hard day of cave exploring you can immerse yourself in a warm stream or rock pool and wonder what the Indian artists ever saw in these palm-shaded canyons.

For information and bookings contact Oscar Fischer at **La Posada Motel** in San Ignacio; in the U.S. call *Baja Expeditions* at (800) 843-6967, or *Off the Gringo Trail* at (800) 344-8890. Both run multi-day trips.

Loreto to San Javier, and Beyond...

Though a 39km (24mi) dirt road connects Loreto and San Javier, it's also possible to walk the distance, following an old mission road down the bottom of a canyon, beneath palm trees, and beside a little stream. Some say that San Javier's mission, started in 1699 and completed in 1758, is the finest in Baja. For a small tip a caretaker will show you around. Because of the aridity and isolation, the building's moorish-style structure is remarkably well preserved.

From San Javier the Mission Trail runs as a poor rocky road to Comondú, the site of another Jesuit mission, set deep in a watered valley between dry, barren mesas of volcanic rock. From here, with occasional help from the locals, you can follow the trail north from oasis to oasis as far as you want. Though there is a surprising amount of water at these higher elevations, you might want to hire a local guide, or maybe even hire or buy some pack animals. During the last part of my walk detailed in my book *Into a Desert Place*, after much haggling I bought a burro for US$30.

Todos Santos to Sierra de la Laguna
by Jim Conrad

Orientation

This hike begins in downtown Todos Santos, takes you across 20km (12mi) of hot desert, and then during a steep hike takes you up through various vegetation zones to a wonderful forest-surrounded meadow that's cool (or cold), moist (or soggy) and thus completely unlike anything you'd expect to find in Baja.

During the climb, the view toward the Pacific becomes more and more spectacular; during most of the climb you'll hear surf breaking on the beach 25km (15mi) away. Borderline cloudforest toward the top is populated by a slender yucca and curiously gnarled oaks with low-hanging branches heavily festooned with gray-green lichens. One conspicuous bird is the orange-eyed junco, which really has bright-orange eyes, and which is so tame that you can get within 3m (10 ft) of it.

Several hiking options are possible. For instance, from the meadow you can take a trail toward the north that meets a road eventually connecting with Hwy 19. Some people arrange to be met there by someone in a vehicle. Another option is even more intriguing. Why not continue from the meadow toward the northeast, descend the slope on the Gulf-of-California side, and eventually connect with Hwy 1?

After scouting most of the distance down the eastern slope, because of the lack of water, I consider this route too dangerous for any but experienced hikers carrying the best maps. Trails habitually begin looking well traveled, but gradually peter out and end at the edges of cliffs, or inside thickets of excoriating *uña de gato*, or cat-claw acacias. If you do want to hike between the Pacific and Gulf of California, you might consider beginning on the eastern slope. If you manage to make good connections there and reach the top, descending the Pacific slope will be a piece of cake.

If you're hiking this route any other time than during the northern winter, you may want to forgo the 20km hike in the desert; even in the winter the desert can be awfully hot, and no water is to be found. On the other hand, the desert's plants and animals are delightful. Giant cacti rise 6m (20ft) high, there are Joshua-tree-like yuccas, and cholla and barrel cacti, as well as such desert-loving birds as the endemic black-fronted hummingbird, scrub jays, ladder-backed woodpeckers, cactus wren and ash-throated dove.

The sandy road connecting Hwy 19 with the entrance to Sierra de la Laguna usually carries at least two or three pickup trucks a day. Since people in these parts are very helpful and friendly, you *may* be able to hitch all or part of the way — but, especially during the fiery summer, you shouldn't depend on serendipitous offers. In Todos Santos you can get information about hiring horses and mules at **The Todos Santos Inn** at no. 17 Obregón. One fellow approached me on the highway offering $15 chauffeur service. Of course, coming back across the desert is another problem. If there is a full moon during your visit, making a night-hike might not only be reasonable, but also an exquisite experience! Just watch out for rattlesnakes!

Once you're across the desert, water (needing purification before drinking) is available at the headquarters at the mountain's base, again at a nice camping spot midway to the top, and at several streams coursing through the forests and meadows at the peak.

In the winter it's possible for the cloud-choked peak to be locked

Desert Survival

by Graham Mackintosh

Between April 1983 and March 1985 I hiked around the entire coastline of Baja, south from San Felipe on the Gulf side, and south from Ensenada on the Pacific side. My goal was to survive off the sea and the desert. My diet consisted largely of fish, shellfish, crabs, seaweed, cactus, cactus fruits, rattlesnakes, and whatever I could obtain from ranches and fishcamps. I rarely went hungry. Obtaining drinking water was always my prime concern.

Temperatures in Baja from May to September are hot everywhere except in the immediate vicinity of the Pacific coast and the very highest elevations. Midday temperatures often hover around 38°C (100°F). When it's that hot the Baja backpacker should always be aware that *your life expectancy without water is about 24 hours* (assuming complete rest). You need to drink almost continuously and must budget a minimum of 4 liters (one gallon) of water a day. Don't venture anywhere in Baja without adequate supplies of water, or knowing exactly how you're going to obtain it.

On my journey I would regularly go four or five days without seeing anyone or finding a water source. Then I would have to make my drinking water from the sea. I carried three different types of still. The first was an inflatable solar still made by Airborne Industries of Leigh-on-Sea, Essex, England. It was described thus in a survival products catalogue: "SOLAR STILL. Specialised inflatable unit designed to supply the occupants of a liferaft with 0.5 to 1.5 litres (½qt to 1½qt) of fresh water a day through solar evaporation of seawater. Can also be used on land. Weighs 0.9kg (2lb)"

My most important still cost less than $10 and consisted of a kettle, a cork and length of aluminum tubing. I would boil seawater in the kettle and condense the steam by passing it through the tubing. By tending this still through the evenings and long midday breaks I could make several gallons of drinking water a day. There was normally plenty of driftwood or dried cactus for a fire.

The third type of still was the classic desert still comprising a polythene sheet spread over a freshly dug hole in the ground. The sun draws the moisture from the soil, water droplets form on the underside of the plastic sheet and run down to drip steadily into a collecting vessel placed underneath. A good daily yield would be less than a liter.

Even with these stills I came close to dying of thirst on at least three occasions when forced inland by impassable cliffs. Without access to seawater my stills were practically useless. Don't imagine you are going to get enough water from cacti — you have to find water or make your way back to the sea!

Graham has written a book about his experiences, Into a Desert Place. *See Bibliography.*

in cold drizzle for distressing periods of time. No matter how silly it seems when you're in the hot, sunbaked lowlands, carry warm clothing to the top.

Getting There

Todos Santos is easily available via buses departing from La Paz's main terminal. Note that the main terminal is *not* the terminal located near La Paz's tourist office, next to the bay, shuttling ferry passengers to Pichilingue. About half an hour of pleasant walking from downtown brings you to the main terminal. Anyone can point your toward *el terminal central de autobuses*.

In Todos Santos buses deposit you next to the Parque los Pinos which, significantly, is equipped with a pump discharging allegedly potable water; the following trip description begins at this park. If you need to stock up before taking off, follow Hwy 19 away from the park — toward Cabo San Lucas — and climb the hill to the high-priced but well-stocked, *gringo*-oriented market called Super Mercado Hermanos Castro. Other *mercados* in town may be cheaper, but their selection of items is severely limited.

During the winter Todos Santos crawls with North Americans, especially in the vicinity of the Super Mercado Hermanos Castro. Here people fill their vehicles with groceries, go down to the park and fill plastic jugs of water, then drive a few kilometers to the beach, where they park, and then enjoy free camping for remarkable periods of time; Todos Santos's seaside ad-hoc campgrounds constitute a true socio-economical phenomenon.

Logistics

La Paz, an extremely pleasant town and, at least away from the beach, quite Mexican in flavor despite its touristic status, offers about 25 lodging places rated with one to five stars, and several no-star places. In Todos Santos the one-star *Misión Todos Santos* is located at Juárez y Márquez de León; but don't forget the nearby, eminently campable beach and wide-open desert.

The Trail

Leaving Parque los Pinos, walk along busy Hwy 19 toward the southeast. Half a kilometer up the road you pass Super Mercado Hermanos Castro, and about 1km (0.6mi) farther, for the meantime ignore the sign pointing to the right, reading *Acceso a la Playa.*" About 2km on down Hwy 19, atop a ridge, you begin your 20km (12mi) trip across the desert by embarking upon the gravel/sand road departing on the left.

During the entire 20km walk you'll see the highlands looming before you in the east; just keep walking toward them. One settlement is reached by an access road branching off the main route. It's well marked with signs, and you don't want to go to there. The main place you might possibly get confused is about 5km (3mi) into the desert, where the road splits. Take the road to the left and continue toward the peaks rising in the east.

At the park's entrance you'll see a gate and probably some loafing soldiers from the nearby army base. If later you're walking along the road in the park's lowlands and hear a vehicle behind you, you'll do well to vault out of its way; the fellows drive those big trucks like you'd expect young guys with big engines to drive.

A sign at the park's entrance advises visitors to check in at the headquarters. However, there's no hint as to where headquarters is, which is unfortunate because water is supposed to be available there.

After entering the park, about ½km (⅓mi) farther the road splits and a sign points to the left saying, *Camino a la Sierra de la Laguna*. Taking this left, about 2½km (1½mi) farther a trail breaks off to the left, next to a sign reading *Subida a la Sierra de La Laguna*, which is the trail we now embark upon.

Once you're on the trail, becoming disoriented is practically impossible. Just keep following the trail upward during six or seven hours of hard climbing. About midway you reach a fine place for camping and most of the time, if not always, there's even a stream here with water in it. Unfortunately, livestock roaming the slopes above the stream preclude the water from being pure. However, if you use as much of your water as I did crossing the desert and then climbing upward for half a day, you'll be glad to see that water, and when you smell the water you'll be glad you can purify it.

Reaching the top, after a brief descent you enter into an open meadow with frog-filled water-seepages draining into small streams. The air is delightfully cool and moist, if not downright cold and wet; unfortunately, wherever there's accessible water, nearby there are also mushy piles of cattle poop.

The main camping area, a meadow or pasture much larger than this one, lies about ½km (⅓mi) farther down the trail. Just keep on the main trail and before long you'll pass by the ranger's hut standing next to a luscious meadow about 1km (⅔mi) long and half as wide, surrounded by plenty of valleys and hills to explore.

Chapter 7

The Copper Canyon Area
(Barranca del Cobre)
by Steven Vale

GENERAL INFORMATION

Few backpackers venturing into the Sierra Madre Occidental come away disappointed; this range provides some of the best hiking in Mexico. Formed many thousands of years ago, the Copper Canyon part of the range has been carved from a vast plateau in the southwestern part of the state of Chihuahua. Of the many tribes that lived here some 2,000 years ago, the Tarahumara, Tepehuan, Pima Bajo and Varohio (or Guarojio) remain. The most numerous group is the Tarahumara, of which there may be around 40,000; the Tarahumara's running ability is legendary.

GETTING THERE

The lovely train ride between Los Mochis on the west coast and Chihuahua brings you into the Copper Canyon area, with a 20-minute stop at El Divisadero for the superb view of Urique Canyon. By land from the U.S., the best entry point for Los Mochis is at Nogales, south of Tucson, Arizona. From Los Mochis, the best connecting Mexican bus lines are Tres Estrellas de Oro and Transportes Norte de Sonora. Tickets for the train in Los Mochis can be bought from the travel agent next door to the Santa Anita Hotel; you'll probably need to spend at least one night in Los Mochis. Beware of getting ripped off the following morning if you take a taxi to the station (it's too early for the buses).

About every 20 minutes Chihuahuenses and other bus lines run

Sierra Tarahumara

Bocoyna
Sisoguichi
Creel (2338m)
Sanchez
Laguna Arareco
Panalachi
Recohuata
△ 2522m
Río Conchos
Río Tararécua
Basuchi
△ 2666m
El Divisadero
Río Urique
Barranca del Cobre
Guahuebo
Guahuachique
Río Urique
Cerocahui
2358m △
A. CerroColorado
Urique
Laguna de
Aboréachi
La Bufa
Batopilas
(501m)
Tónachi
Río Batopilas
Río Fuerte
Río San Ignacio
Agua Blanca
roads
Río San Miguel
rivers and lakes
Ciénega
Prieta
railways
settlements
Barranca de Sinforosa
continental divide
Río Verde
N
0   15   30 kms

from Ciudad Juárez (across the border from El Paso, Texas), from the Central Camionera; it takes 5 to 6 hours to reach Chihuahua. It's possible to reach Ciudad Juárez by bus from inside the U.S. by crossing the border with Chihuahuenses buses. These leave hourly from the El Paso Greyhound terminal. If you are delayed at the border, keep your ticket, as it is possible to use it on the next bus.

The train station in the city of Chihuahua, Ferrocarril Chihuahua al Pacífico, is at Calles Méndez and 24. Sometimes it's possible to book tickets by mail; write to the Superintendencia General de Tráfico at Depto. de Fletes y Pasajeros, Apdo. Postal Num. 46, Chihuahua, Chih. Mexico). Probably 99 percent of travelers buy their tickets the day before departure from the station.

If you plan to stop in Creel I recommend making the first part of the trip by bus, not train, because buses are much quicker and more frequent. The bus station is located on Calle Progresso and has a good restaurant on the second floor. Buses leave almost every hour for the 5hr trip.

Note: All of Railway Route 220 operates on Central Time — you must remember this in Los Mochis, which is on Mountain Time, one hour earlier.

WHERE TO STAY

There are two main hikers' centers in the area — Creel and Batópilas. In Batópilas places to stay include **Posada Monse** and **Hotel Batópilas**.

The small town of Creel, at an elevation of 2,338m (7,672ft) provides the easiest access to Copper Canyon's main hiking areas — Copper Canyon (Barranca de Cobre) as well as the other canyons of Urique, Sinforoza and Tararecua. Creel's fame increases from year to year. **Margarita's Guest House** is hugely popular, and there are several other fine places. At Margarita's a bed in the dormitory, with breakfast and evening meal, costs US$3.50, while double rooms with private bathrooms go for around $18.

Alternatively, a new hostel provides bunk-bed accommodation and camping facilities. Called **Camping — Sierra Madre Camping Group's**, it's a converted ranch with a river nearby for swimming. The building is situated about 8km (5mi) from Creel and, according to Eduardo Miledi at the Parador de la Montaña, a vehicle will meet guests from the train. Cost is about US$16 per person, which includes breakfast and evening meal. There's good hiking in the area and a number of horses are available for hire. To make reservations contact Ofincinas Centrales at Calle 7ª No. 2810, Chihuahua (Tel: 15-00-57).

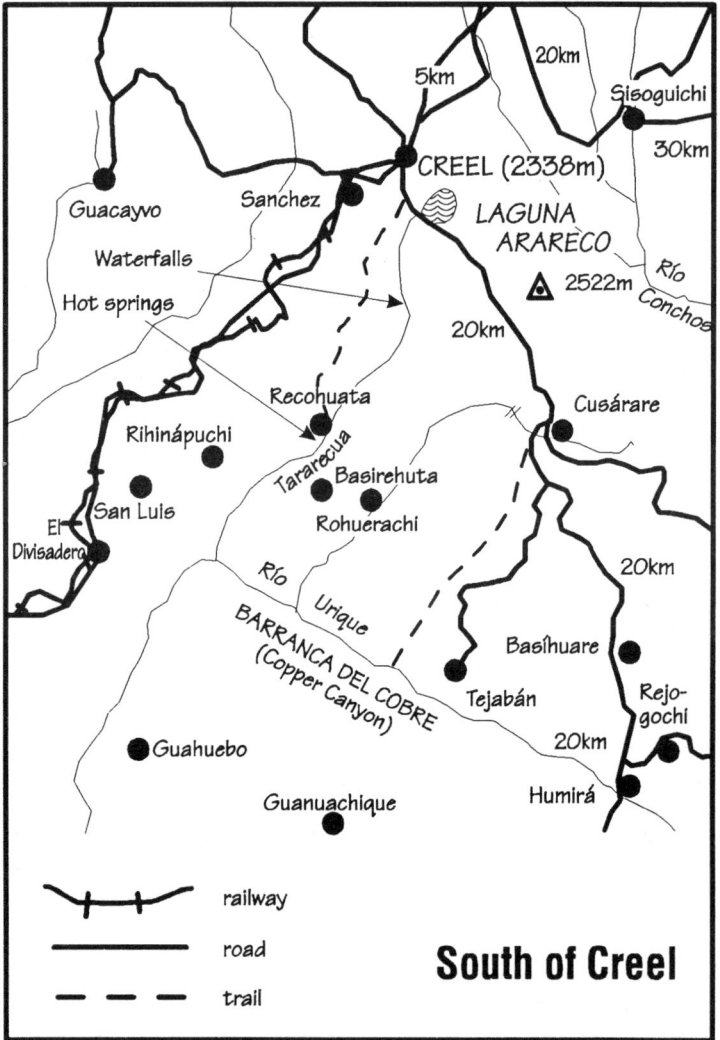

South of Creel

Guacayvo

5km

20km

Sisoguichi

30km

CREEL (2338m)

Sanchez

LAGUNA
ARARECO

Waterfalls

2522m

Río Conchos

Hot springs

20km

Recohuata

Rihinápuchi

Tararecua

Basirehuta

Cusárare

San Luis

Rohuerachi

El
Divisadera

Río
Urique

20km

BARRANCA DEL COBRE
(Copper Canyon)

Basíhuare

Tejabán

Rejo-
gochi

20km

Guahuebo

Humirá

Guanuachique

railway

road

trail

HIKES AROUND CREEL

Warning

At these elevations the strength of the sun should not be underestimated. After soaking for about 3hrs in the hot springs mentioned in the next hike I suffered from sunburn for three days. And carrying a heavy pack on a burnt back does not make for good hiking.

Hot Springs Hike

This easy hike provides two full days of walking, plus a chance for further exploration of Tararecua Canyon; you can also continue into Copper Canyon and proceed to El Divisadero.

The dirt road leading to the canyon is found about 9km (5½mi) outside Creel, along the paved road to Cusárare. You might want to spend the first night at Lake Arereco, about 5km (3mi) out of Creel, on the left side. Easy to reach on foot, it offers secluded campsites at the far end, and great swimming if you like cold water; numerous Tarahumara rock shelters can be seen to the right of the paved road. Supposedly you can hike around the lake in anything from 5 hours to a whole day. I tried walking to the right of the dam wall and had to turn back after reaching a forestry project fenced off with barbed wire. Better camping possibilities can be found by crossing the dam wall and walking around the lake shore. Hitching in the Creel area is easy, though you normally end up sitting in the back of a pick-up truck.

After spending a cold night at the lake it's possible to walk the remaining 3km (2mi) to the hot-springs turnoff, which comes before the km10 marker. About 500m (⅓mi) past the km9 post the road bends sharply to the left and after a further 100m (330ft) there is a yellow road sign on the left (seen with Creel behind you). Continue along the paved road a further 100m until on the right there's a wide dirt road. This leads through the pine forest, with piles of rubbish on both sides. Though you encounter various forks, the main track is easy to follow — especially in the wet season, when 4-wheel drive imprints will result from organized tour groups.

Rock formations during the early part of the walk are interesting. The dirt road passes over several rockbeds before passing the only meadowland in the area, to the left. After ⅔hr walking there is a three-fork junction. After continuing straight, a canyon becomes visible directly in front.

By the way, on this road one day we thought we had stumbled across a forest fire because we saw a column of smoke rising from among the trees in front. However, it transpired to be a huge fire in the middle of the road, with no-one in sight. Some tour operators had hired a fellow to keep the road operational for 4 X 4 vehicles; the fire had been built upon protruding rock which, when heated sufficiently, became brittle enough to break with a sledgehammer!

Continuing, the road starts descending and after a number of switchbacks eventually turns a sharp right, leaving a small farm below, to the left. From here it is a further 1 to ½hr to the canyon rim. Here the 4 X 4 track ends, but a single path continues across a stream (during the wet season it may be running), and through the trees.

From here good rock formations can be seen on the opposite side; to the right the canyon curves out of sight to where it eventually encounters Copper Canyon. To continue into the bottom of Tararecua Canyon and to Recohuata Hot Springs, take the steep track leading between the rocks to the right of the viewpoint. There are several shortcuts, which in addition to offering a steeper and quicker descent, also encourage erosion. Snakes inhabit this canyon; I surprised one, and visa versa, about halfway down. All routes eventually arrive at a point about 50m (165ft) above the river, which at this point consists of large pools filled by short waterfalls.

Keep the river to the left until the path descends to the water level. Here it is easy to cross, even in the wet season. A couple of faint trails lead down to a single log bridge where the river must be crossed again. This can be a traumatic experience during the wet season! Excellent swimming holes lie to the right of the bridge. The main trail continues downstream, passes a derelict house and arrives at a purpose-built thermal bath which is about ½m deep by 2m in length (1½ by 6½ft). This is a great place to sooth aching muscles; it contains the hottest water in the area. Alternatively, leave the bath to the right and continue downstream to the river (which needs to be forded), where a further 100 to 150m (330 to 500ft) downstream is a sort of natural water-slide, plunging into a deep, cold-water pool. Though during the rainy season water in the river is likely to be cold and murky, in the dry season the river's pools are not likely to be so large, but they'll contain warmer water from the springs.

At this midway point, the best camping areas are to be found around the derelict house; ample firewood is available. Allow a full day if you plan to hike out to the main road via the steep climb out of the canyon. During the dry season the river contains the only water in the area; in the wet season numerous streams pass along the access road. It is advisable to purify all water before drinking.

Variations

Daniel at Margarita's offers day-trips costing $9 per person (minimum 8 people); it may be possible to take the outward or return journey with him, if he has a group going.

I'm told of the possibility of hiking from Hot Springs to the bend in the Urique River, where it enters Barranca del Cobre. Here a path leads to El Divisadero, where you can catch the train back to Creel or onto Los Mochis. This is likely to be more of a dry-season hike, as flash floods during the rainy season will make crossings difficult. Allow ⅔ day from the hot springs. Backpackers hiking this route would probably do better to start from El Divisadero, due to the difficulty in finding the path to the hotel from below, whereas the hot springs are easily recognized.

According to Patrick Foley, it's possible to follow the river from Lake Arareco into Tararecua Canyon. Unfortunately, Patrick never made it to the hot springs because he was unable to find a route around one of several waterfalls. Here is a description of his attempt:

"The river always has water in it, because it is fed by Laguna Arereco. It is also fed by the Arroyo de Creel, so be sure to purify your water. The river is easy to walk along and there are trails and even a dirt road for a few kilometers. You enter the arroyo 3km (2mi) south of Creel, near a couple of ranchos where corn, sheep and deforestation are featured. The people seem shy, but if you visit the area during local festivals (particularly Easter) you will observe religious processions and sacramental inebriation! As you head south, the creek bed drops gently or abruptly. After about 5km (3mi) you reach one of those waterfalls you see in the movies about the Andes, and you cannot follow the creek anymore. Camping is possible nearby (watch out for flash floods), or you can scramble up to the plateau above which is lightly forested with pines, oaks and junipers. Here we found what looked to be coyote scat full of juniper berries. The topographical map suggests paths east and south on the plateau which are worth investigation, but if you keep to the canyon rim you will have no problems finding your way. One effort to descend the canyon walls south of the waterfall ended with a tumble. To continue, ropes would be a great help."

Maps

The canyon is featured on the 1:50,000 Creel and San Jose Guacayvo map and on the 1:250,000 San Juanito map. Both are available from the Mission Store in Creel, though they were out of stock during my visit.

COPPER CANYON

Orientation

Although Copper Canyon is the best-known canyon in the Western Sierra Madre, it's one of the least visited; most travelers see it only from the rim at El Divisadero, where the train stops for 15 minutes.

Copper Canyon is at its deepest point almost 2,300m (7,550ft) below the surrounding plateaux. Various settlements have been established on terraces in the canyon where apples and peaches, as well as staples such as corn (maize) are grown. The Río Urique flows through Copper Canyon before entering Urique Canyon, where it continues past the town of Urique and into the Río Fuerte.

This is a tiring 3-day hike requiring a whole day to reach the canyon rim and a further day needed for the return trip to the Urique River. With sufficient food supplies it is recommended to spend one or two rest/exploring days in the Canyon bottom before beginning the return journey.

I have heard of one or two travelers who have tried, unsuccessfully, to find the route alone only to spend one or two nights totally lost before finding someone to point them in the direction of the road to Creel. Therefore it is advisable to hire a guide for this hike. I recommend Sr Reyes (normally his son serves as the guide), who charges about $15 a day — excellent value when split between a group. We also hired two burros at $5 each per day, which were a great asset in the dry season for carrying the large quantities of water required. To contact Sr Reyes, who lives in the Cusárare area, speak to Margarita at Margarita's guest house in Creel.

Bring food for 4 to 5 days; it's impossible to buy anything en route. Although the guide brings his own tortillas he appreciates any extra food. A hat is essential and bathing costume useful for swimming in the Urique River.

Getting There

The easiest way to join up with the guide is to take the 7am bus from Creel to Batópilas, which departs on Tuesday, Thursday and Saturday. The bus leaves about a block away from the Chihuahua bus office; confirm the departure time with Margarita. Sr Reyes will arrange to meet you somewhere between the Cusárare and Tejabón turnoffs, which lie 20 to 25km (10 to 15mi) from Creel.

The Trail

After meeting Sr Reyes we were taken to his house where
backpacks and water were loaded onto burros. The first day is then
spent traveling along the dirt road to Tejabón, following the guide,
who speaks no English, as he deviates from the route taking
memorized shortcuts. There are limited views the first day. After 7 to
8 hours of walking you will leave the pine forest behind and views
into several canyons will open up. The trail continues to follow the
dirt road until the guide takes a right through an assortment of
boulders before arriving at a number of small corrals in the middle
of which is a derelict house.

At this first overnight stop there are plenty of good campsites. For
anyone without a tent the disused house provides a roof for the
night. Our guide simply wrapped himself in a blanket and slept
beside the fire. There is ample firewood in the area and a fire is
almost an evening necessity in both dry and wet seasons, as the
temperature drops sharply after sunset.

At the far end of the corral directly in front of the house is an old
well that in the wet season can be relied upon for water. During my
visit in April it contained about 3 litres (3qt) of murky water and we
were forced to buy (!) the precious commodity from a nearby house
for about US$2.

The overnight area is about an hour's walk from the canyon rim.
The trail skirts around pine forest before crossing what appears to
be a 4 X 4 route where the trail descends steeply to the left. Shortly
the first views of canyon's bottom become available, the Urique River
showing up as a faint, meandering line.

High on the opposite side of the canyon and tucked into a terrace
is the village of Huacaybo and on the steep descent it is not unusual
to meet villagers carrying huge loads of firewood, maize or fruits. For
these people the hike to the highway, which would take us almost
two days, is a mere day stroll, even when heavily laden.

Allow 2 to 3 hours for the descent, which follows a well-marked
trail and eventually arrives at a small section of forest, where the trail
splits. The left fork leads down to the river and the chance to cool off
in clear waters. There are a number of disused houses to explore in
the vicinity and the lower canyon sides are dotted with a number of
caves made by gold prospectors; one of these lies a short way
upstream, on the opposite side of the river. Locals still look for gold
in the canyon and it is not unusual to hear the steady beat of a rock-
hammer high in the rocky outcrops.

It's possible to spend a few hours in the bottom of the canyon and
still make it back to the previous night's camping area; this is
convenient for anyone wishing to make this a 3-day hike. Those
backpackers with more time will be well rewarded if they spend a

night on the river bank, which in the dry season affords some excellent, sandy campsites. Driftwood for fires abounds.

Another option is to travel up the opposite hillside with the guide, who has many friends in the village.

The return journey to the paved road can be made in one long day, where it is possible to hitch a lift back to Creel without too much trouble.

Variations

It may be possible to find a 4 X 4 owner willing to take a group of hikers to El Tejabán in the dry season; I couldn't find anyone prepared to undertake the trip in the wet season. Ask around in Creel for Pedro who drives a green Ford pick-up; he's supposed to charge the cheapest rates.

Maps

The Mission Store in Creel sells a 1:50,000 map of Samachic covering both the canyon and the approach. It costs US$2.

Warning

It is foolish to attempt this hike without the use of a guide. Other travelers have reported that, although it is easy to ask the way in the early stages, the remoteness and confusing number of trails in the latter stages make the chance of reaching the canyon rim quite remote, with the likelihood of ending up totally lost.

Day-Hike to Sisoguichi Mission and San Ignacio

There are numerous half- and full-day hikes in the vicinity of Creel; good trails lead off in almost all directions. Perhaps the best known is the 6 to 7 hour round-trip hike to the Catholic mission of Sisoguichi and the village of San Ignacio. This easy hike also provides good opportunities to see not only Tarahumara cave dwellings but also the Tarahumara themselves traveling the route to Creel.

To get there simply follow the main street in the direction of Lake Arareco, past the liquor store and the lumber mill to where the dirt road forks. Take the left fork, which continues towards the cemetery (The right joins the main highway). Keep to the right of the cemetery and the first cave dwellings can be seen on both sides of the road about 1km (⅔mi) out of Creel. The ores mined in these canyons during Colonial times went on the backs of burros in such numbers that in places trenches were worn into bare rock.

The Mission of Sisoguichi was founded in 1676, and is still active. A convent atop a hill overlooks two valleys which join here. Both in San Ignacio and Creel it is possible to buy tiny baskets woven from 20cm-long (8in) Chihuahua-pine needles, as well as white-wood violins, which the Indians have made since the Spanish introduced the instrument. These violins are now used in religious services.

Instead of returning via the same route, Janet Bishop suggests continuing about 2km (1¼mi) past the church at the ejido's crossroads (in the direction of Gonogochi) until a trail is reached heading north into the forested uplands. An easy 2km hike leads uphill to a ridge with good views. This is a good camping area; no-one lives in the area. Water can be taken from a creek below the ridge.

From the ridge continue north where you need to scramble over numerous rock formations before returning to farmland. To return to Creel, head west and find a notch in the ridge just east town. If you get lost, as with other hikes in the vicinity, local farmers and giggling children should soon put you right. Good views of Creel reward anyone reaching the final ridge by sunset.

Batópilas to Urique

Allow between 7 to 10 hours in a packed second class bus to cover the 140km (87mi) from Creel to Batópilas, which has a population of 600 people, and an altitude of 501m (1,643ft). In Batópilas cows, pigs, donkeys and chickens wander freely through the main street; any swimming in the Río Batópilas should be done upstream from town because of untreated sewage entering the river.

A hike that I have not done yet is recommended by Eduardo Miledi of the Hotel Parador de la Montaña — a three-day hike from Batópilas to Urique. Apparently there is considerable steep uphill walking and unless one of your group is an excellent map reader, a guide is needed; Timo Loya, who lives in Batópilas, has been recommended. He charges from US$15 to $25.

From Urique it is possible to get a lift with the post van to Cerocahui though I am told that this may take one or two days. From Cerocahui there are buses to Bahuichivo, which lies on the main rail line between Los Mochis and Chihuahua City. A second-class train in each direction makes a daily stop. Allow at least 7 days for this trip.

Day-Hike between Batópilas and Satevo

Though this hike following the Batópilas River downstream is easy, travelers report that in May daytime temperatures can rise unbearably high. One reason to visit the tiny settlement of Satevo is to see its 500-year-old church. Soon Sativo's isolation may end because renewed mining activity in the area may result in the construction of a dirt road. The hike back to Batópilas is best done in the early evening.

Parque Natural Cascada de Basascachic

This area, about 140km (87mi) by road from Creel, lying toward the northwest, is said by some to offer the finest hiking in the country. One of its waterfalls plunges 310m (1,017ft) in a single, unbroken cascade, making it the tallest in North America. Camping is possible at a public campground. Trails connect the end of the road to the top of the waterfall — a distance of about 3km (2mi). Supposedly a trail from here passes through the woods, eventually reaching the town of Basascachic; other hiking possibilities exist in the area.

The park can be reached from Chihuahua by taking either bus or train to La Junta. From here it is 130km (81mi) by road. From Creel, go to San Juanito and then, as with the approach from La Junta, expect a rough bus journey.

Chapter 8

Other Hikes in
Northern Mexico

EL SALTO TO LA CIUDAD BY ABANDONED RAILROAD ROADBED
by Jim Conrad

Orientation

Years ago someone decided to build a railroad track connecting Durango and the Pacific Coast. From the beginning everyone knew it'd be a monumental task because the tracks would have to pass from northern Mexico's central plateau, across the Western Sierra Madres, to the Pacific Coast. About midway between Durango and Mazatlán, just west of La Ciudad, the railroad would come to the plateau's brink and then precipitously, scenically and wildly plunge all the way to the lowlands.

Building westward from Durango, at El Salto the railroad builders met their first deep canyons — vertical-walled gorges reminiscent of Copper Canyon's abysses. At first, by snaking the track back and forth atop a west-jutting tongue of the plateau, they managed to keep the track more or less level. However, near La Ciudad, at about 2,600m (8,600ft), finally they had to dive toward the lowlands. Just beyond the lovely waterfall known as Mexiquillo the builders began blasting a roadbed for the track down a canyon's wall; on the right rose a near-vertical rock wall; on the left opened stomach-churning emptiness.

Six tunnels were dug before the project had to be abandoned. Too many workers were dying from accidents and even before any

The Ferry between Baja and Mainland Mexico

by Jim Conrad

Most guidebooks give the impression that acquiring a ticket for the ferry between Baja and the mainland is a maddening process, but that, once you find the ticketing place, the cost is low. I haven't found ticket-buying any more maddening than other things in Mexico, and the tickets aren't particularly cheap.

Though maps generally show several ferry routes dotting the Gulf of California, in early 1992 there was only service between La Paz and Mazatlán, La Paz and Los Mochis (port of Topolobampo), and Santa Rosalía to Guaymas. Though schedules change from time to time, just to give you an idea of what might be expected, here are the ferry times in 1992:

	leaves	arrives
La Paz to Mazatlán	1500	0800 next day, no Saturday boat
Mazatlán to La Paz	1500	0800 next day, no Saturday boat
La Paz to Topolobampo	2000	0600 Tuesdays only
Topolobampo to La Paz	1000	1800 Tuesdays only
Guaymas to Santa Rosalía	1100	1800 Tuesday, Thursday & Sunday
Santa Rosalía to Guaymas	2300	leaves Tues, Thurs & Sunday 0600 next day

In Mazatlán tickets can be bought at the ferry terminal, which is about an hour's walk from downtown, or ten minutes by city bus. (To ask which number bus you need to take, say *¿Puede usted decirme qué número tiene el autobus que va al terminal de barcos? Quiero irme a La Paz.*)

In La Paz ferry tickets are sold downtown, not far from the tourist information office next to the beach, at the travel agency known as SEMATUR, at Guillermo Prieto y 5 de Mayo. La Paz's ferry terminal lies about 20km (12mi) north of town, at Pichilingue; throughout the morning and early afternoon buses leave La Paz for Pichilingue nearly every hour. The bus station serving Pichilingue is not the same as the main bus terminal. In La Paz the bus station serving the ferry terminal at Pichilingue lies across the street from the tourist information office along the beach. The main bus station serving other locations in Baja is about a half-hour walk away (*¿Donde está el terminal central de autobuses?*).

Three kinds of ferry tickets are available — *salón, turista* and *cabina. Salón* provides access to a fairly spacious parlor equipped with tightly packed, airplane-type reclining seats. *Turista* puts you in a smaller room with more personal space; *cabina* gives you access to a cabin. Prices change regularly, but in early 1992 a one-way *salón* ticket cost about US$17.

In Santa Rosalía and Guaymas ferries leave from the town harbour.

If you're crossing the Gulf on a budget, one way to avoid being sardined into the big *salón* is to get aboard early during the loading process, ignore the seat number on your ticket, and head for the rear of the ship, where during the night you can stretch out in a sleeping bag on benches bolted to the wall. Don't forget your sea-sickness medicine; even calm crossings generate unsettling swells.

In La Paz, in the vicinity of the tourist office along the beach, walk inland a couple of blocks and you'll find yourself in *el centro* among numerous pleasant, reasonably priced hotels. Even in Mazatlán there are inexpensive, un-touristy places. Across from the bus station and only three blocks from the beach, for instance, **Hotel Economica**, which is tolerably clean and even has hot water if you're among the first in the morning or evening to bathe, costs only US$10.

tracks were laid avalanches were burying huge amounts of work. Just beyond the sixth tunnel the project was abandoned. Today the unfinished railroad-roadbed from El Salto all the way to Tunnel 6 near La Ciudad is good only for walking...

Only at the very beginning and very end of the abandoned roadbed is the scenery spectacular. The first kilometer out of El Salto follows the rim of a canyon; the last three or four kilometers descend a canyon's wall. The approximately 30km in between course through pine and oak/pine forests, pastures, through little villages and alongside ranches.

Midway the hike, just outside Las Adjuntas, the trail crosses from the northern side of Mexican Hwy 40 to the southern side. Since the hike's first half, on the northern side, is more populated and disturbed than the second half, misanthropes — and those unwilling to cross the abandoned trestle mentioned in the trail description — have the option of bypassing the trail's first half by taking the bus to the midway point. Tell the bus's ticket-taker you want out at Las Adjuntas, where the old railroad crosses the highway — "*Quiero bajar en Las Adjuntas, donde el ferrocarril viejo cruce la carretera.*" If the ticket-taker doesn't know about any railroad, just disembark at Las Adjuntas and hike back toward Durango, to the top of the hill. Remember, you won't be looking for tracks, because they were never laid down; you need an abandoned roadbed. Several families live in the area so you can always ask for directions — "*¿Donde está el ferrocarril viejo?*" Remember to trill your *rr*'s.

Though I found the people around El Salto to be friendly and helpful, I was a little unnerved by the number of individuals who volunteered the information that I stood a good chance of being robbed around El Salto. Therefore I didn't yield to the strong temptation to peg my tent at the brink of the canyon just outside El Salto.

By the way, this hike was discovered by accident when I visited El Salto to scout the Parque Nacional Puerto de Los Ángeles y Barranca de Los Negros, which on many maps is portrayed as a vast hunk of land immediately south of El Salto. Some touristic literature refers to El Salto as the park's gateway. Unable to find a road to the park, I visited El Salto's municipal building, where the town's fathers had never heard of the park. Apparently Parque Nacional Puerto de Los Ángeles y Barranca de Los Negros is more of a bureaucratic entity than a developed destination.

During 99% of this hike there can be absolutely no doubt as to where the roadbed is; it's the notch they've dynamited through the ridge, the elevated levee passing across the marsh, or the only level place on the side of a vertical rock wall. Sometimes, however, as when you pass through a settlement or where logging roads cross the trail, if you don't pay attention you can wander off the trail. When in doubt, return to the last point where you were sure you were on track, turn around, and then project the roadbed before you.

By "projecting" I mean to keep in mind that trains never make sharp turns or begin climbs or descents quickly. Their roadbeds always make ample turns and the beginnings of their climbs and descents are hardly perceptible.

Between Las Adjuntas and La Ciudad, you pass through some tunnels in which a flashlight becomes useful, if not indispensable.

Getting There

El Salto is easily accessible with the many buses plying Hwy 40 between Mazatlán and Durango; the Estrella Blanca line offers several departures a day. Most buses leave in the morning in order to have the steep grades behind them before nightfall.

Where to Stay

In El Salto itself, which stands at Km 100, buses stop right beside a rather seedy looking, mud-spattered, nameless hotel. At Km 80, east of town, a *centro recreativo* called **Paraíso de la Sierra** rents cabins in a sylvan environment. Just west of El Salto the hiking trail passes through the town of 1010 — pronounced Mildiez. A dirt road connects Hwy 40 with 1010. Mexican tourist literature mentions cabins and trout fishing available at 1010; when I passed through it was miserably cold and rainy and my mood was as bad as the taciturn locals, so I can't vouch as to the cabins' presence. At this time there's considerable talk about building tourist facilities beside the falls of Mexiquillo near La Ciudad.

The trail

From the unnamed hotel right beside Hwy 40 in El Salto, walk along the road in the direction of Mazatlán. In about three minutes you'll cross a bridge over a small river; running along the river below you'll see the railroad track. Once you're across the river, descend to the right and take the dirt road paralleling the track. This is the only part of the hike where crossties and steel rails mark the old roadbed.

Enjoy the majestic scenery during the first kilometer out of El Salto because by the Kilometer Two you'll already be traveling overland, passing across pastureland that during rainy periods can be awfully soggy. In fact, in some places where the railroad's culverts have collapsed, you may have to get your feet wet. Beyond the pasture lies the town of 1010. The roadbed passes through town heading more or less northwest; it exits along the left (southern) side of a picturesque valley.

About 1km (⅔mi] beyond 1010 a trestle about 15m (50ft) high and 25m (80ft) long crosses a rambunctious stream. The trestlework is solid but there's no proper surface to walk on; you must tread sturdy planks held in place by wire; naturally there are *no handrails*. If for 25m you can maintain your balance on a 0.8m-wide (2⅔ft) plank surface over fast-moving white water, you'll have no trouble. If you're acrophobic and your pack isn't too big, probably you can scoot or pull it and yourself across, collecting only a few splinters.

For most of the next 3km (2mi) the roadway courses through a pretty valley populated with scattered houses. After about 8km (5mi) the trail approaches but does not cross Hwy 40, and you traverse the community of Lechería, which consists of a couple of soft-drink-and-cracker eateries, but no place offering real meals. After four or five more kilometers, during which most of the time you're within earshot of the road, you cross Hwy 40 on the northeastern side of the village of Las Adjuntas.

Beginning the part of the trail lying south of Hwy 40, you have smooth sailing for the first 2½km (1½mi), but then you come to a tunnel about 300m (980ft) long. During my rainy walk the tunnel's lower end was flooded. However, concrete barriers about 35cm wide and 50cm high (1ft wide and 1⅔ft high) inside the tunnel rose above the roadbed, and at about a distance of 35cm paralleled both of the tunnels' walls for the entire distance. By creeping atop the submerged barriers while keeping a hand against the wall to steady myself, I negotiated the tunnel without getting too wet. In places the submerged barrier tops were slick with mud; just take your time.

Maybe 0.7km (½mi) farther you come to another tunnel, but it's no sweat. About 3km (2mi) father the roadbed once again approaches Hwy 40 and you cross a rather well maintained gravel road. Approximately 15km (9mi) after Las Adjuntas you come to the smallish but picturesque waterfall called Mexiquillo. Here you can take the footpath on the fall's left side (left, standing in front of it, looking at it) and shortly come to La Ciudad, which has several fine roadside restaurants, but which is short on good lodging. Noticing that the railroad's roadbed continues beyond Mexiquillo, and that now you're returning into some gorgeous scenery, you may do as I did, and simply keep following the roadbed.

Tunnels 3 and 4 are not long in coming, but they are easy to get through. Tunnel 5, however is impassable; you must go around it. Thus as you approach Tunnel 5 notice that to the tunnel's left a trail snakes across the slope toward the far exit.

Shortly after Tunnel 5, Tunnel 6 comes along. I was told that it's possible to pass all the way through this one and continue briefly on the other side, but to me it looks too dangerous to fool with. It's very long, with rocks fallen from the ceiling and, most of the time, flooded rather deeply. Once again there's a trail angling across the slope, departing from the left side of the tunnel. Avalanches have practically obliterated it so it's a bit hard to locate and follow; if you can just hack through the first hundred meters or so, soon you'll come to an overgrown access road that apparently once connected Tunnel 6's entrance with the slope's top. Locating the road, just follow it upward; when you come to a park-like place at the end of a ridge, the road zags back toward the right, continuing upslope.

Arriving atop the plateau you'll find several logging trails coming together; take the one heading southward at 160°. Follow the road as it winds generally toward the north and west. After one or 1.5km (a bit less than a mile) you'll be following a bearing of 280° when you encounter a crossroad. La Ciudad lies about 3km (2mi) to the right, but if you're planning to camp in the woods overnight before catching a bus in the morning you may prefer to take the left leading off at 200°. About 400m down the road you'll come to a little farmstead called **Rancho el Venado**. The folks living here, Raymundo and Gloria Zapata, and their kids, will sell you a cup of coffee for about 75¢ and, if they have the fixings, even provide you with a full meal. The Zapatas grow their own corn, beans, squash, potatoes, chickens and cattle.

Returning to the crossroads, this time taking the right toward La Ciudad, after 2km (1¼mi) you come to a large sawmill with a fence around it. If there's someone to ask, it's easy to take a shortcut through the sawmill; however, on the other side signs tell people to stay out. Without an invitation, probably it's best to skirt the sawmill by following the gravel road along its northwest side.

La Ciudad is a hard-working, muddy, sprawling, raucous, fairly ugly town with nice roadside restaurants catering to truckers. A bus station is housed in an obscure building with no signs announcing its presence; just ask for the *terminal de autobuses*.

TAMÁN TO XILITLA
by Jim Conrad

Orientation

In two days you can easily make this trip, which has a good deal of sustained but not drastically steep climbing in it. A peaceful camping area occurs along a beautiful, isolated stream, the Río Tanquilín, midway along the walk. Even during the rainy season the Tanquilín can be crossed by wading across fast-running waters a little over knee deep. However, don't attempt this hike immediately after very heavy rains; give at least a couple of days for the waters to subside. During the winter the ford's waters stand only about knee deep. After rains this trail can be miserably muddy. Keep in mind that limestone, the region's dominant rock, is treacherously slick when smeared with mud.

This hike is different from most because it passes through "heartland Mexico." It's not inside a park or across an isolated mountain chain, nor does it connect with an archeological ruin or any other touristic destination. This walk through Gulf-Slope, humid mid-elevations uses "Indian trials" and rudimentary roads that carry you into villages hardly ever visited by outsiders. Most of the people met along the way speak Nahuatl in their homes. You'll meet farmers on their way to work in their much-eroded hillside cornfields, and regular people walking cross-country, just to save the cost of a bus ticket. The Nahuatl speakers tell me that their trails have been in use since before Montezuma (the Aztec king when the conquistadors arrived) and that may be the truth. Nahuatl, is very closely related to Aztec, which Montezuma spoke.

By the way, I've written a nature-and-Indian-oriented book about this area. If you're interested in getting a feeling for the area before you go, take a look at my *On the Road to Tetlama*, published by Walker and Company of New York in 1991.

Getting There

You really have to spend the night in a hotel in order to get an early start the next day and to do this you need to go to Tamazunchale, a small but bustling town in the extreme southern corner of the state of San Luis Potosí; it's at the very foot of the interior plateau's Gulf Slope, about 300km (185mi) by road northeast of Mexico City. Situated on the Pan American Highway, dozens of buses pass through every day. The main busline serving the area is Flecha Roja.

How to Make a Nahuatl Speaker Smile

by Jim Conrad

On the hike between Tamán and Xilitla, pay attention to how Nahuatl speakers shake hands with one another. The usual Mexican handshake is a three-step operation beginning with a regular US/European shake instantly followed by a "mutual wrist-grab" like the "black-power handshake" seen in the US back in the '60s and '70s, instantly followed by another regular shake.

Most Nahuatl men know about this shake and will expect you to shake hands in that way, but among themselves they prefer something else. They hold out their hands in the usual way but, before clasping, the hands pause so that just the fingertips gently and fleetingly touch. The extreme contrast between the rambunctious Mexican shake and the tentative Nahuatl shake points to the profound dissimilarities and conflicts that must have characterized relations between the early Spanish settlers and the native Americans who became their slaves and servants. It also causes me to be on my guard against seeming too aggressive when I'm among them, and being too disruptive of their traditional routines.

I get a kick from the Nahuatl-speakers' surprise and delight when I offer them their own kind of shake. If you want to throw them for an even greater loop, try these Nahuatl sentences on them, pronounced in the Spanish way:

Good afternoon, sir. = *Tiotlaquilti tate*
What are you doing? = *¿Tlachqui quichihua?*
See you tomorrow. = *Hasta mostla.*
Have a seat. = *Ximosehuica.*
I want some beans. = *Nijnequi etl.*

Where to Stay

The most pleasant place to stay in Tamazunchale is at the **Quinta Chilla**, which has its name painted on the wall between it and the highway, about ½km south of town; a double room costs about $12.00. In Tamazunchale several hotels along the main drag provide the usual fare; I find them too close to the loud highway for my liking. If you're looking for a cheap place that's as colorful as it is seedy, from anyplace along the main highway through town head down to the park. On the first through-street heading north, look for the **Casa de Húespedes**, offering double rooms for about $7.50.

Around 7am *colectivos* begin running between Tamazunchale and Tamán, and Tamán is our next stop; the trip costs about US35¢. During my last visit they thought they might change the departure

location so just ask, *"¿De donde salen los colectivos para Tamán?"*
In Tamán stay in the *colectivo* all the way to the end, to beneath a
fig tree several blocks off the main highway.

The following trail begins at this fig tree. However, when you arrive
there you well may find a pickup truck parked beneath the tree, with
Indians milling around, looking as if they're waiting for something.
They're waiting for the truck to carry them to Agua Zarca, your next
major destination; the truck will leave when it has enough
passengers. Passage costs about US$1.75 and in the truck it takes
about 1¼hrs. Walking, maybe 6 or 8 hours.

Going in the back of a pickup truck may not be a bad idea. Most
of the trip to Agua Zarca is steeply uphill, the first half is particularly
weedy, and most of the time it's quite hot. Also, if you hike the entire
distance occasionally stopping to enjoy the scenery, you may not
reach the Río Tanquilín camping spot, which lies beyond Agua
Zarca, before darkness falls. One option is to ride halfway; that'll
bring you into the cooler highlands and you'll still get to walk
through the best scenery. To ask to be let out halfway, say, *"Quiero
bajar cuando llegamos a medio camino porque quiero caminar
cuando hay una vista buena."* If you arrive at the fig tree and there's
no pickup truck waiting, you can begin walking and maybe later flag
down someone. Between Tamán and the Río Tanquilín, there's no
lodging and no good place to camp (the wooded slopes are too
steep) unless you ask someone in Agua Zarca if you can rent a spot
in their front yard where you can peg a tent.

At the trail's end, one of my favorite camping spots lies not far up
the road from Xilitla. It's in a cool to cold, high-elevation pine forest
with widely spaced trees creating a park-like ambiance. At Xilitla's
bus terminal buy a ticket to *el Entroque de Tres Lagunas*, which is
nothing more than a road intersection in the forest a few miles west
of El Madroño, on the way to Jalpán. There's plenty of interesting
forested landscape around the crossroad, so you may want to stock
up on groceries before heading there. Xilitla and the *entroque* lie on
Hwy 120, the main road between Tampico and Querétaro, so you
seldom need to wait long for a bus.

The Trail

This trail begins at the fig tree (American fig with elliptic leaves, not
Old-World fig with three-lobed leaves) surrounded at the base by a
concrete wall about 0.5m (20in) high, next to the general store called
the "Mini Todo." If you're hiking, take the street running west at 295°
all the way to the end, cross the bridge, and simply continue
following the gravel road all the way to Agua Zarca. Toward the end
you'll pass a town in the valley below, to the left, but that's not Agua

Zarca; Agua Zarca is well announced with signs declaring its population to be about 2,500. If you arrive in a pickup truck you'll be deposited at the basketball court; if you arrive walking, head for the same court.

Walk across the court and take the big trail heading 320° up the hill. Atop the hill continue down the main fork to the right, bearing due north. During the next minutes of walking keep in mind that your general plan is to descend the valley opening toward the north-northwest from Agua Zarca. Dozens of small footpaths will branch off the trail, but just stay on the main one, and keep in mind that you're heading NNW. It wouldn't hurt to occasionally confirm your navigation by asking, *"¿Es éste el camino al Río Tanquilín?"*

About an hour after leaving Agua Zarca's basketball court you'll be in a very weedy agricultural area and the trail will suddenly fork and rise; take the left fork. You'll know you've taken the correct path if at the top of the 5m (15ft) rise you see that the two trails are connected by a shortcut trail, so that a triangle, with sides about 10m (30ft) long, forms around the mound. If you like this kind of hiking you should know that if you'd take the right fork you could eventually arrive in Tamazunchale, or even farther north, in Matlapa... You'll further be confirmed that you're OK if the left branch you're taking leads off at 300° to the northwest.

After the fork, as you descend toward the river, the trail bifurcates several times. Each of the three times I've walked this trail, by the time I could hear the Tanquilín's waters I was simply guessing as to which fork to take. Approaching the river I was always sure I'd become hopelessly lost and thus would be at the wrong place in the river. However, each time, as if by magic, I reached the river at exactly the same spot. This is good evidence that, at least after the 5m mound, most or all of the trail's forks eventually reconnect before the river is crossed. Nonetheless, as you descend it wouldn't hurt to pay attention to the general lay of the land; usually on the trail's lower section there's no one to ask directions from.

When you come to the Río Tanquilín you'll certainly want to know whether you've really arrived at the right fording place. If you have, the following details should be true:

The river should be flowing toward the WNW, at 300°. Right below you, the river should make a hard curve to the right. Across the Tanquilín, at a bearing of 220°, you should see a white limestone boulder about 2m (6ft) in diameter. At least when the water is low, a bar composed mostly of cobblestone is in front of the boulder. If these details aren't correct, then you'd better backtrack.

Because of the nice breeze and view, I usually camp on the cobblestone bar. If you prefer to put your tent in deep shade and on a softer, more regular substrate, probably the best place is on the river's Agua Zarca side. Return inside the forest and walk downstream a few meters. You may even be lucky enough to spot some stones that are part of an ancient Indian ruin.

Ford the stream by crossing where you first met the river and walking more or less toward the limestone boulder; the path to Xilitla begins a few meters to the left of the limestone boulder, and runs diagonally up the slope, toward the northwest, at 325°. For the next 2km (1mi) it's mostly uphill, generally heading toward the north. The first settlement you'll enter is Poxtla, which at first is more audible than visible — roosters crowing, turkeys gobbling, babies crying, and battery-powered radios playing *música tropical*. Eventually Poxtla crystallizes into a real settlement with a dirt road but no electricity and no restaurant, though there are some cracker-and-beer kiosks.

From Poxtla continue upslope for about 3km (2mi). During the climb's final stage you'll notice buildings before you clustered high in a gap between two hills. Finally arriving at this gap you'll probably have mixed feelings about reentering the realm of rural electrification; one of the buildings you've been seeing is a general store with ice-cold Cokes; but the peace and quite of the Río Tanquilín now lie far behind. The town announced by the general store is Cruz Titla. The next 3km up the road gradually bring more and more urbanization, until finally atop the slope you step onto Hwy 120, on the outskirts of Xilitla.

Slash and Burn

by Jim Conrad

When I walked between Tamán and Xilitla for the first time in the mid 80's, slopes in the vicinity of the Río Tanquilín constituted a veritable wonderland. Giant strangler figs festooned with gardens of bromeliads and orchids kept the slopes' soil in place; chicozapote and mamey trees — the royalty of rainforest fruit-trees — were common.

By 1992 only scraps of the original forest were left, the rest having gone the way of firewood; I hope that when you arrive you'll see something other than cornfields, for cornfield-planters follow firewood gatherers. No matter what shape the land is in when you visit, it's important for people like us to see what's happening to the land.

During my last visit I asked a *campesino* whether any government programs regulate use of the region's forest or keep the steepest slopes from being converted to highly erodible cornfields. "*No, no hay nada de eso,*" he replied — "There's nothing like that." I'm sure that elegant land-use programs do exist on paper but, in the field, as you'll see, *no hay nada.*

PEÑA NEVADA
by Jim Conrad

Orientation

This hike has two main attractions. First, the trip to Peña Nevada takes you through some very interesting, traditional Mexican towns seldom visited by foreigners, as well as some very fine desert scenery; second, Peña Nevada itself is so isolated that at this writing its forests are not yet completely destroyed. Peña Nevada is a 4,054m (13,303ft) peak in the Eastern Sierra Madre range.

Though the Spanish word *nevada* means "snowed-on," usually Peña Nevada is snowless. Nonetheless, I managed to conduct my scouting trip during a week in February when snow did indeed fall. Near the top I found myself slogging through a knee-deep accumulation, unable to find my trails. It's hard to simply look at Peña Nevada and know if there's snow on top. Snow quickly melts on the western slope, which we see as we approach the peak, because intense afternoon sunshine melts it; but on the unseen northern and eastern slopes, beneath the tall pines, snow can linger for days. Because I didn't make it to the top, the trail description supplied here brings you almost there, but then you're left on your own! The trail described is easy to follow and there's little chance you'll loose your way.

When the locals hear that you're planning to visit Peña Nevada nearly always they open their eyes very wide and say, "*¿Y los osos?*" — "And the bears?" Everyone talks about the bears atop Peña Nevada, and a few people who never take a step off the *rancho* honestly find the idea of going there terrifying. Happily, most of this bear-talk is just good-natured kidding; if people get the impression that you're really starting to worry (and eventually you do), they'll laugh and admit that the bears almost always, as soon as they see a human, run away. *Almost* always...

Getting There

The closest town to Peña Nevada regularly served by buses bears the odd name of Dr. Arroyo. Dr. Arroyo lies about 50km (30mi) east of Matehuala, which is between the larger cities of Saltillo and San Luis Potosí. Though Dr. Arroyo is accessible from the north by Hwy 61, certainly the most direct route by bus is via Matehuala. Matehuala is a sprawling, fairly modern and common-looking town;

its new bus terminal, too far from *el centro* to make a nice walk, offers connections with Dr. Arroyo on a nearly hourly basis throughout the day, mostly on the Transportes Tamaulipas bus line. You'll like Dr. Arroyo; it's about as sun-baked and somnolent as a town on a main road can be, and the people couldn't be more friendly.

Dr. Arroyo's bus station is situated next to a pleasant park, some small general stores, and a fruit store. Closer to Peña Nevada you'll have a chance to stock up again, unless it's *siesta* time, too early or too late in the day, or if there's some kind of *fiesta*. If you arrive in Dr. Arroyo during the day, neither very early in the morning nor too late in the afternoon — that's as specific as I can be! — next to the park opposite the bus station you should spot some pickup trucks or *colectivos* parked in the shade. If you don't see "Peña Nevada" written on one of the vehicle's windshields, ask if any of them do go there. The Peña Nevada referred to on the windshield refers to the town of San Antonio Peña Nevada, lying a few kilometers west of the peak of Peña Nevada.

The bumpy trip to San Antonio takes a little over an hour, the time depending on how many chores the driver must deal with. You'll probably see him deliver mail along the way, relay produce from one little settlement to the other, and engage with people standing along the road in the most complex-sounding conversations. Though the gravel road continues beyond San Antonio into the mountains, *colectivo* service ends at San Antonio. If you were pleased with Dr. Arroyo's sunburnt, dusty, and friendly character, you'll be thrilled with San Antonio.

Where to Stay

Though in the village beyond San Antonio you can buy saltine crackers and *refrescos*, San Antonio's general stores are the last well-stocked ones along our way. My favorite acquisition there were some large bags of crispy, chili-powder-covered, very cheap taco shells. Of course there are no hotels in this area, but the desert is big enough for fine camping.

The Trail

The *colectivo* ride from Dr. Arroyo to San Antonio is mostly downhill, entering a huge valley paralleling the western slope of the Eastern Sierra Madres. San Antonio lies in this valley's trough. Thus in San Antonio as you begin hiking the gravel road toward the peak, you immediately begin climbing. However, it's a gradual climb and you pass through some spectacular desert — one of the greatest concentrations of Joshua-tree yuccas I've ever seen. Also there are many large barrel cacti, pricklypear cacti, leg-stabbing lechuguilla and medicine-smelling creosote bush. It's 6km (4mi) from San Antonio to the next small village of Santa Lucía; you see Santa Lucía at the range's very base as you walk toward it.

During your progression toward Santa Lucía take a good look at Peña Nevada's slope rising before you. The trail described here takes you by gravel road to a high gap maybe 5km (3mi) to the left (north) of Peña Nevada, which is the highest peak. Notice that several trails can be very clearly seen running up the slope. The locals say that to reach the peak one trail is about as good as the other, that all of the paths starting at the bottom lead to the same place on top, and vice versa. Many of these trails are made by men with horses who climb from the desert to the forested peak, chop down one tree, and then drag it back down. If instead of continuing on the gravel road trip I'm describing you prefer to ascend via one of the trails climbing straight up the slope, the option is open. Since during nearly the whole climb you'll be able to look over your shoulder and see San Antonio in the valley below, becoming disoriented for any length of time is unlikely.

From Santa Lucia it's about 14km (8½mi) by gravel road to the previously mentioned gap, known as El Puerto. You needn't be embarrassed about taking the gravel road when much more difficult and direct routes are available; the road, at least at this writing, sees only two or three vehicles a day, and the scenery is very pleasant. Before being hit with the snowstorm, my plan had been to take the road to El Puerto, then after visiting the peak, descend on one of the steep trails ending at Santa Lucía, and that still seems like a good plan. However, I ended up walking the road twice, and enjoyed both coming and going.

You'll know you're at El Puerto when the road suddenly levels out and you're at a Y, with one arm heading 350° and the other 20°. At west 90° you'll see a small log cabin. You want to pass to the left of this cabin, climb up behind it, and continue on the foot-trail leading up the valley. At this time there's a cornfield not far to the right of the cabin; you need to pass between the cabin and the cornfield. In the vicinity of the cabin the trail is obliterated by livestock paths leading off in every direction; just keep heading toward the east-running valley behind the cabin and soon you'll discover the main trail, perfectly clear by frequent traffic consisting of horses pulling logs downslope. Not far up the valley you'll enter a very interesting forest rising only to about 5m (15ft) high, consisting of red-barked madroños, a thick-trunked species of yucca different from the one in the desert below, and scraggly oaks with branches heavily laden with lichens.

About half an hour after El Puerto the trail zags hard to the left, but soon begins arcking back toward the east, following a bald along a ridge. Then a fine, almost level trail leads below the pines, gradually begins climbing, veers to the northeast, and atop a small ridge eventually hits a road. Again, all roads and paths lead to the same place, I'm told. Keep watching your compass.

It was at this point in my own journey to the peak that the snowstorm hit and I was unable to continue...

Mexican fan palm

92

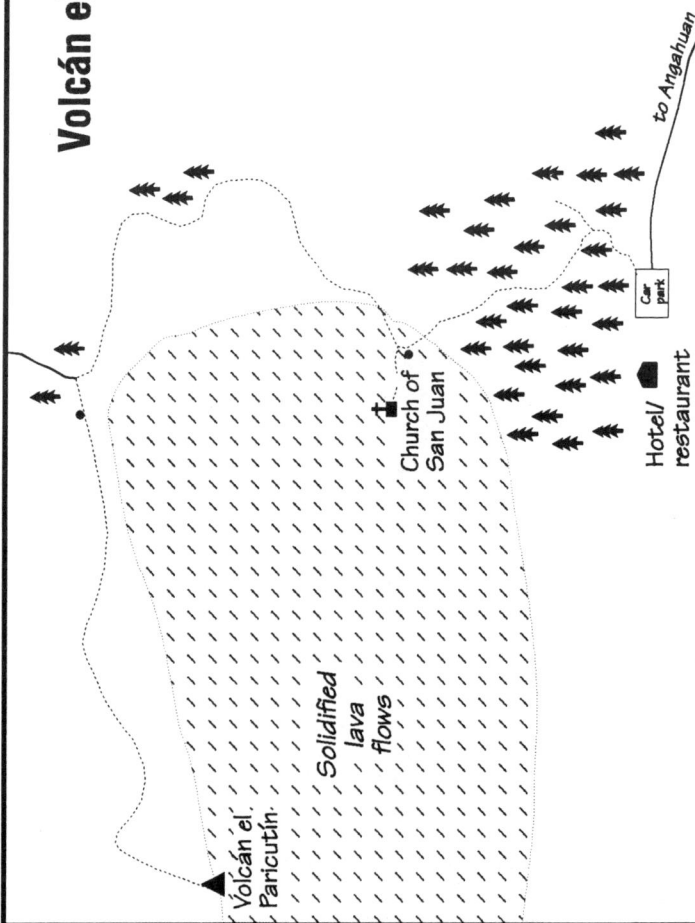

Volcán el Paricutín Hike

Key:

——— dirt roads

········· trail

solidified lava

• bottled drinks available

🌲 pine forest

Volcán el Paricutín

Solidified lava flows

Church of San Juan

Car park

Hotel/ restaurant

to Angahuan

Chapter 9

Central Mexico's Volcanos

by Steven Vale

VOLCÁN EL PARICUTÍN

Orientation

In the state of Michoacán, about 500km (300mi) by land due-west of Mexico City, just west of Uruapan, Volcán el Paricutín rises to an approximate height of 2,785m (9,140ft); my maps seem to be in disagreement about just how high it is. Whatever its precise height, it's not terribly lofty, and can be classified as an easy two or three-day hike. There's plenty of infrastructure in the area for volcano-climbing tourists, so this qualifies as a good trip for novice volcano-climbers.

Getting There

Uruapan, the closest major city to Volcán el Paricutín, is served by first-class buses from Mexico City, Guadalajara, Morelia and other places. Uruapan itself has lost some of its earlier charm, but a number of reasonable hotels and restaurants are still clustered around the main plaza.

At the Central Terminal you can store any luggage you don't want to lug up the volcano for about US30¢ per bag per day. Buses to your jumping-off place, the town of Angahuán, depart about every two hours, and the trip takes approximately an hour. Tickets for numbered seats are on sale 30 minutes prior to departure. If possible ask for a seat on the bus's left side so that on the way there you can enjoy a good view of Paricutín. Those catching the

5:30am bus will be grateful for the station's 24-hour cafeteria.

Arriving in Angahuán, a horde of guides with horses will probably meet you at the bus stop; prices for guide services vary enormously. I was quoted US$30 when I left the bus but by the time I'd reached the *zócalo* it had dropped to $10. Eventually we made a deal for $20 for three people, and that included a guide. One way to avoid the hassle with the guides is to leave the bus at the access road to Angahuán about 500m (⅓mi before the main stop. A sign on the right (Volcán Paricutín Angahuán) points to a paved road on the left leading to the plaza; there's a white tourist-information kiosk at the junction.

From the main bus stop simply follow the only road into town. Keep the plaza to your left and at the new wooden house take the dirt road to the left; electrical lines follow this route. After about 40 minutes the road ends at a hotel where several luxury chalets, or *cabañas*, have been built. Some afford views of the volcano.

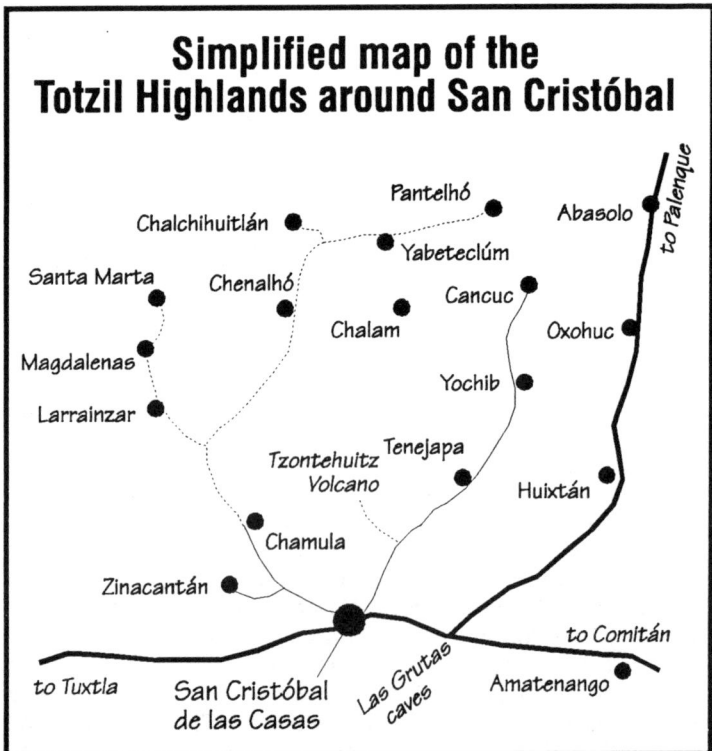

Simplified map of the
Totzil Highlands around San Cristóbal

Pantelhó

Chalchihuitlán

Abasolo

to Palenque

Yabeteclúm

Santa Marta   Chenalhó

Cancuc

Chalam   Oxohuc

Magdalenas

Yochib

Larrainzar

Tzontehuitz   Tenejapa
Volcano   Huixtán

Chamula

Zinacantán

to Comitán

to Tuxtla   San Cristóbal   Las Grutas   Amatenango
                 de las Casas   caves

Where to Stay

Reservations for this hotel, known as **Misión Morelia**, can be made by contacting Hospitales 145, Colonia Vasco de Quiroga, Morelia (Tel: 2-36-58). A *cabaña* for six people costs $25; the hotel's restaurant serves a filling *comida corrida* for about US$2.

The Trail

The trail begins by leading to the church of San Juan, which from the hotel's terrace can be seen. Take the trail leading from the right of the parking area before the hotel. After a steep initial descent the trail flattens and forks. Take the wide left path; the hotel should now become visible perched on the ridge above. After about an hour the trail arrives at the edge of a lava field, skirts it along the right, and then forks, with the left fork going across the lava to the church, and the right continuing on to Paricutín. At this fork a shrewd local has set up a bottled drinks stand. He'll tell you that it's a 7-hour roundtrip journey to the crater.

From the fork a number of trails and 4 X 4 tracks lead off in different directions, though all routes seem to convey us to the same ash road. If in doubt, the numerous groups of horses plying the route normally leave a clearly visible trail. After about 30 minutes the road forks, but later reunites. Follow the ash road for 1 to 1½ hours from the fork, sometimes passing through groves of avocados and apricots.

At some point a barbed wire fence crosses the track — this is easily unhooked to gain access. Eventually the road cuts back towards the volcano just as you pass the last lava flow and think that you are going too far to the right. To confirm that you are on the correct path there should be a couple of buildings within 100m (100yd) on the right side. Bottled drinks are for sale here.

Even 4 x 4's can get by here, skirting the lava flow's edge. Eventually the road enters onto a wide ash bed flanked by forested hills to the right. Continue following the horse tracks; after a further 45 minutes the uphill section starts. Allow yourself 4 to 5 hours after leaving the bus to reach this point.

Though camping is possible anywhere on the broad ash bed, choose your spot carefully in the wet season for there are numerous water run-off channels. The good thing about camping one or two hours from the crater rim is that with an early start (take a flashlight) you can watch the sunrise in solitude; the guided horse-trips don't start arriving until much later.

The final ascent, via the ash slope on Paricutín's right side, takes anywhere from 30 to 60 minutes. From the top there are superb views of the solidified lava flows spreading out like huge tentacles

Popocatépetl and Ixtaccíhuatl

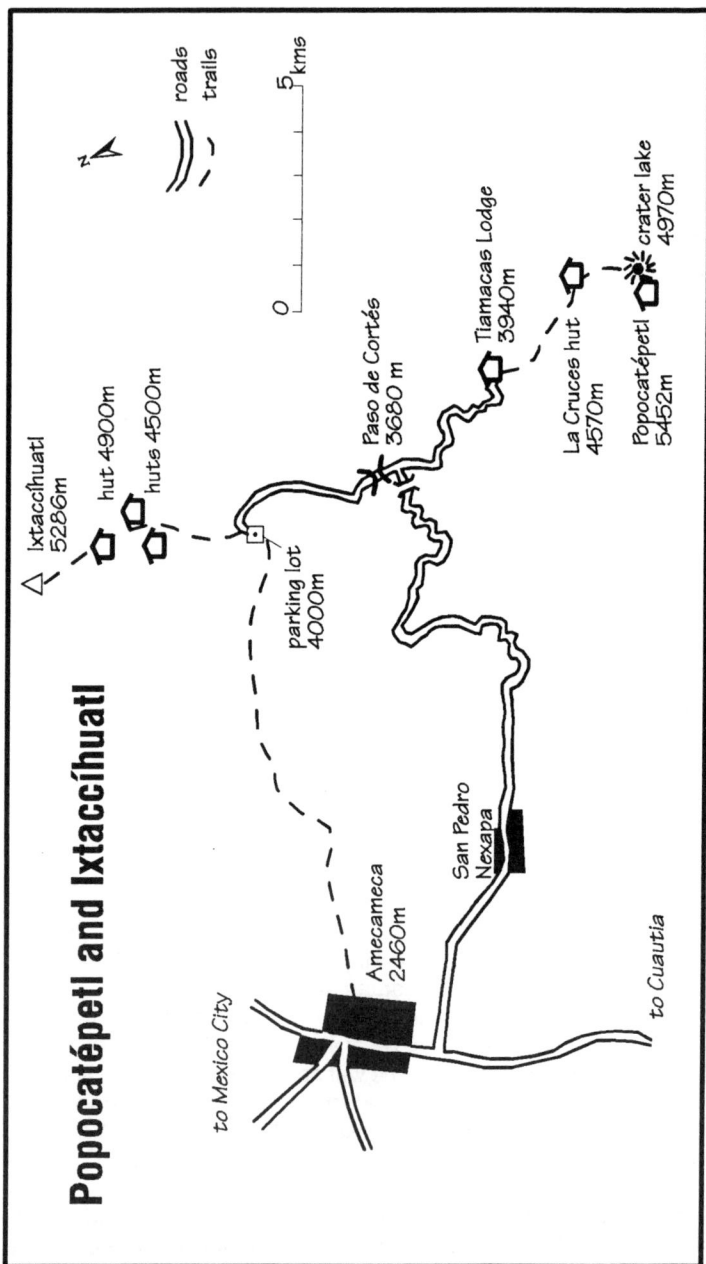

roads
trails

5 kms

N

Ixtaccíhuatl
5286m

hut 4900m

huts 4500m

parking lot
4000m

Paso de Cortés
3680 m

Tlamacas Lodge
3940m

La Cruces hut
4570m

crater lake
4970m

Popocatépetl
5452m

San Pedro
Nexapa

Amecameca
2460m

to Mexico City

to Cuautla

across the valley. We were fortunate to witness a thunderstorm as mist blotted out the surrounding hills and steam gushed from fumaroles around Paricutín's base.

Warning

Don't make the mistake of seeking a more direct route to the crater across the lava field. The solidified lava is like a dry coral bed — walking on it is hard on boot soles and ankles.

POPOCATÉPETL AND IXTACCÍHUATL

Orientation

Popocatépetl — Popo to its friends — soars 5,452m (17,891ft) high, thus ranking as Mexico's second-highest mountain (Orizaba, also known as Citlaltépetl, reaches 5,700m (18,705ft). Nearby Ixtaccíhuatl — Ixta — comes in third at 5,286m (17,346ft). The names are Aztec; *popocatépetl* means "smoking mountain" and *ixtaccíhuatl* translates to "sleeping lady" or "white lady." Since Popo-Ixta National Park lies only 60km (37mi) from Mexico City, Popo and Ixta are the most frequently climbed peaks over 5,000m in Latin America. However, don't let this information imbue you with a false sense of security; people have lost their lives on these climbs because of falls and sudden snowstorms.

Since this book is for backpackers rather than serious mountaineers, our trail description is for the relative simple Las Cruces route. Experienced climbers will find the Ventorrillo and Grietas routes more interesting; further information on these can be obtained at Tlamacas Lodge, or from the book *Mexico's Volcanoes* (see *Bibliography*).

Warning The importance of gradual acclimatization can't be stressed enough. During my stay several travellers raced up to Tlamacas Lodge from Mexico City and attempted the ascent early the following morning. None successfully reached the crater rim, complaining of nausea and double vision. All had to make a hasty retreat back down to Amecameca due to bad headaches.

Volcanic Rabbits Popo-Ixta Park is home to a unique animal — the Zacatuche — best known as the Volcano Rabbit. It is only found on the upper slopes of the two mountains. It is smaller in size than a normal rabbit, is dark brown, has short ears and a small tail. Though it is a protected species its numbers are on the decline, mainly due to illegal shooting and loss of habitat to agriculture.

Getting to Popo-Ixta Park

The main entrance-town for Popo-Ixta Park is Amecameca — usually pronounced simply as "Ameca." In Mexico City, buses for Amecameca leave from the Eastern Bus Station (at the San Lázaro exit, on the Observatorio/ Pantitlán Metro line). Cristobal Colon buses depart every 30 minutes on weekdays and hourly on Sundays; the ticket costs about US$1 for the 1½hr journey.

There's an excellent Saturday market across the square in Amecameca where you can stock up on fruit for the trip.

In Amecameca mini-bus drivers come looking for backpackers wanting to go to the park; they charge US$9 for the trip, regardless of the number of people going; 4 or 5 people with heavy backpacks are generally enough. There is no weekend mini-bus service. Immediately after entering the park you come to Paso de Cortés, a high saddle between Popo and Ixta, at 3,680m (12,076ft); a monument commemorating Cortés's first view of Tenochtitlán (the Aztec city that preceded Mexico City; eventually it was conquered by Cortés). The road divides here; straight on goes to Puebla, though this dirt road is in such a bad condition that no vehicles — not even 4 X 4s — use it; right goes to Popo, and left goes to Ixta. The minibus continues to the lodges.

Tlamacas Lodge

Taking the right toward Popo, about 5km (3mi) farther up the road you come to Tlamacas Lodge, situated at 3940m (12,929ft) and serving admirably as a base for climbing Popo. The lodge is furnished with 98 beds; during peak season, use is also made of the huge loft area. Each dormitory (all are mixed) contains about 24 beds with a separate room with toilets and showers. Obtaining warm water can be a problem when few people are overnighting. The lodge also contains a cafeteria where sandwiches, hamburgers and egg dishes are available as well as hot and cold drinks (including beer). Meals in the restaurant upstairs set you back about $5. There's a central lounge area, brightened during winter evenings by log fires. Hikers leaving the lodge before 7am should know that the cafeteria will be closed. On Saturdays and Sundays there are generally enough people leaving early to warrant the cafeteria opening. If you wish to make yourself really unpopular, try banging on the cafeteria door early in the morning. It worked for our group as a sleepy-eyed attendant prepared scrambled eggs and coffee at 5:15am! The restaurant staff are normally a good source of information on the area.

Both crampons and ice-axes can be rented from the lodge's reception area. Current prices, for ageing but adequate gear, are about US$3.50 each piece of equipment per day. The management accepts credit cards as identification and deposit. This also applies to the hire of blankets and sheets; a sleeping bag is advisable for cold nights in the lodge. Luggage can be stored in the small room at the back of the reception area.

A nearby building is the base for Club Socorro Alpino (Alpine Aid Club). Though during the week the building is normally closed, on weekends its members are busy carrying out numerous training rescue operations. Occasionally the members respond to real emergencies (hypothermia is the biggest problem) and if the office is open it is best to register your name, route, and expected return time. You may even be able to join club members on an ascent.

The Trail to Popo

From Tlamacas Lodge several routes lead to Popo's summit. The steeper tracks lead to the Ventorrillo and Grietas routes, which are the more difficult ones. The normal route is via the gently rising ash trail going diagonally left to Las Cruces Hut, which lies at 4,400m (14,439ft); the weather has left this shelter in a pretty sad state. The Las Cruces Hut route is a good one for experienced hikers with rudimentary knowledge of the use of crampons and ice-axe. During summer months I've met hikers who walked to the summit with neither of these aids. Warm clothing and, in the summer, wet-weather gear are essential, however. The hut is reached in 2-3 hours. Reaching the summit is such a straightforward undertaking that no further directions are needed.

The Trail to Ixta

Although Ixta is lower in height than Popo it is a more difficult climb. Ixta is not a simple, cone-shaped volcano like Popo; it's hard to find one's way on this rugged, sprawling, but very beautiful mountain. Maybe you'll be lucky enough to team up with a group; you might check with the Club Socorro Alpino near Tlamacas Lodge.

From Tlamacas Lodge take the road 5km (3mi) back to Paso Cortés. At the park's entrance, where you come to the road leading back to Amecameca, you'll find the last place you can get water on the way to Ixta, the parking lot of which lies about 9km (5½mi) along a dirt road from the monument.

Once at the parking lot, follow the trail as it rises steeply up the mountain for about 15m (50ft) and then flattens out. Continue on this trail for about 3hrs to an overhanging rock often used as a campsite, and for a further 3hrs to the first hut. If this hut is full, notice that downslope about 300-400m (±1,000ft) there's another hut, a red one. As on Popo, all these huts are simple basic shelters with no facilities — but marvelous views. Should both these huts be full (a possibility during weekends), there is a third hut nearly an hour's climb beyond the first two. The huts are all between 4,500 and 4,900m (15,000 and 17,500ft) in elevation. The trail is not always very distinct, but if you keep your eyes open you should be able to follow it by using a combination of red paint-marks, occasional small cairns and wands, the footprints of other climbers and common sense. During cloudy or foggy weather you might have to wait it out.

As you climb you are constantly faced with views of volcanic ridges, sprawling, wild and stupendous. Sheer rock walls jut from the mountain's flanks like the arms of a giant starfish. Huge hanging valleys are draped between them, filled with untold tons of volcanic scree. A hauntingly desolate landscape. Climbing at least as far as the huts is eminently worthwhile for the wonderful scenery alone.

When you reach the snowline follow footprints; the route should be fairly clear except after a heavy snowfall. There are a couple of false summits — the knees and stomach of the "sleeping lady" — but the highest point is on "El Pecho" (the breast) where you will find a huge summit plateau about 500m (⅓mi) long, with the highest point at the north end.

The summit is reached after 6-10hr's climb from the rock overhang (about 3hr less form the huts) depending on fitness, acclimatization and amount of gear. It is not recommended to leave equipment in any hut (Tlamacas Lodge is OK), since chances of theft are high. Most people need at least one night on the mountain to complete the climb, though an ascent and descent from the parking lot would be possible in one long day by fit, experienced climbers with day packs. Allow 4-6hrs for the descent to the parking lot from the summit.

The best time to climb Ixta is in October and November when crampons might be dispensed with, although an ice-axe is recommended as a third point of balance, and for security.

Leaving the Park

The first taxis for your trip back to Amecameca generally start arriving at Tlamacas Lodge around 11am. If going into Puebla, local buses (Micros) depart regularly from Amecameca's *zócalo* for the

20km (12½mi) trip to the Autopista. The bus drops passengers a short distance from the highway, where you need to stay on the right side, with the bridge rising to your left. The best place to stop Puebla-bound buses is from below the bridge (normally there's a group of people waiting). Don't despair if buses roar past; eventually one will stop. The fare to Puebla is about US$1.50. From Puebla's bus terminal taxis cost around US$1.50 for the 20-minute journey to the *zócalo*.

LA MALINCHE

Orientation

This peak, rising to 4,461m (14,639ft) is a popular day-hike; if you have a tent, it also makes a good two-day trip. La Malinche, also known as Matlalcueyetl, is easily visible from Puebla if it's not obscured by clouds during the wet season. No water is available on La Malinche.

Getting There

Long-distance buses carry you to the large city of Puebla. From the main terminal take the Autobuses Surianos line to Huamantla; buses depart hourly. The journey, which essentially takes you from the southwestern side of La Malinche to the northeastern side, passes through the small town of Amozoc, and provides superb views of El Pico de Orizaba, which at 5,700m (18,705ft) is Mexico's highest peak. Allow about 1½hr to reach Huamantla.

Where to Stay

Huamantla is a fair-sized city where last-minute shopping can be done. On the *zócalo* there's accommodation at **Hotel Vallejo**. Day hikers should take colectivos, buses or taxis as far as they can toward La Malinche — to Las Cruces, if possible. Remember that in the evening in Huamantla the last bus for Puebla leaves at 6:30pm.

The Trail

From Huamantla's bus station, walk two blocks along Av. Juárez Sur to the *zócalo*, then embark onto the road leading from the far, opposite corner (Calle Guerrero Norte). Follow this as far as the Pemex station; here, across the street, a road continues towards La Malinche, which may be visible beyond it. This road passes through

Hiking in the Nevado de Colima area

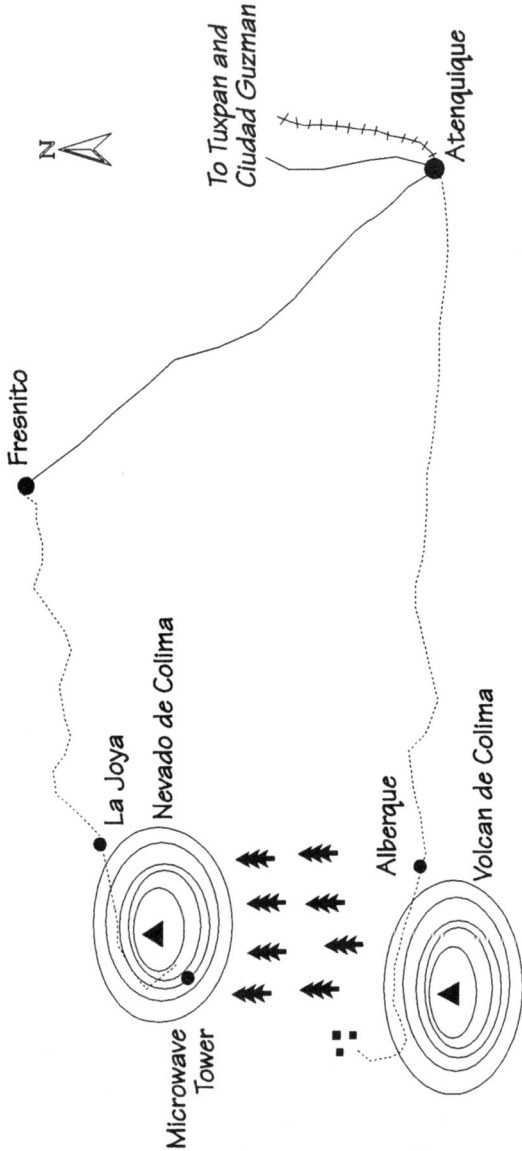

N

To Tuxpan and
Ciudad Guzman

Atenquique

Fresnito

La Joya

Nevado de Colima

Microwave
Tower

Alberque

Volcan de Colima

the small village of Rancho de Jesús and finally the hamlet of Tamira (also known locally as Las Cruces), where a radio mast can be seen about 200m (200yd) up the hill. Up to here the road has been paved. At the next right-hand bend the dirt road leading to the left is the approach road to La Malinche. Day hikers should take a colectivo to this point because, walking to here from Huamantla takes about 1½hrs. A few local buses also serve the villages. Although there is little other traffic, it may be possible to hitch.

Numerous trails depart from the dirt road, leading up through the forest; all seem to wind steadily uphill to the treeline. I chose a trail to the right after walking on the dirt road for about 30 minutes — at a point where the dirt road appears to start descending. Here a single track heads uphill; rights should be taken at each fork. This is a popular haunt for locals searching for magic mushrooms and firewood. Allow about 3 hours to reach what appears to be the lower crater rim. Actually, any number of routes lead to the summit and there are numerous areas suitable for camping, so there's no need to detail any one route in particular.

VOLCÁN DE COLIMA NATIONAL PARK

Orientation

Situated in Jalisco State between the town of Colima and Ciudad Guzmán, Volcán de Colima National Park offers some good hiking on two volcanos — Volcán de Colima and Nevado de Colima. The 3900m (12,798ft) southern peak, Volcán de Colima, has erupted three times this century — in 1902, 1908 and 1913. The northern peak, Nevado de Colima, is extinct, and reaches 4,335m (14,225ft). Most of the park is covered with pine forest, though some of the low-lying gullies harbor lush forests. Rough dirt roads approach fairly close to both peaks, but traffic is so infrequent that you shouldn't depend on being able to hitch a ride. INEGI's 1:50,000 map shows a trail connecting the two peaks; perhaps one of our readers will supply us with the answer as to whether it's possible to take the bus to Fresnito, hike to Nevado, then the Volcán, and return to Atenquique. Nights on these peaks can get quite chilly; during the winter (dry season) it snows.

One-day car trips, which take about four hours each way, can be arranged to La Joya refuge; they cost around $90, so it pays to get a group of about five people together. Cheaper rates can be bargained for a one-way trip to La Joya refuge. A one-way trip with horse and guide works out at about $20 per person from Fresnito to

La Joya. The tourist office in Colima provides a basic map showing the local towns/villages and road distances, together with some information in Spanish. The best map is INEGI's 1:50,000 of Ciudad Guzmán, which shows the routes of the dirt roads to both summits, in addition to connecting trails.

Getting There

By bus, this trip starts in Ciudad Guzmán, about 125 straight-line kilometers 80mi) south of Guadalajara. In Ciudad Guzmán buses for Fresnito leave about every two hours. You can see from the accompanying map that if you want to ascend Nevado de Colima you should stay on the bus until Fresnito, but if you want to hike up Volcán de Colima you need to get out at Atenquique. Beyond the paper-mill town of Atenquique, roads to both peaks are rough, dirt ones.

Volcán de Colima

From Atenquique to this peak the road is about 25km long (15mi). Above the treeline it passes around the northern slope. To reach the volcano's crater, just hike up the pumice slope.

Nevado de Colima

The northern peak, Nevado de Colima, is reached by a 30km (12mi) dirt road which starts on the left side of the road heading towards Los Depósitas, a small village, about 1km (⅔mi) north of Fresnito. This road leads to a pass at 3,800m (12,470ft), where the road turns left along the west slope, toward a microwave station at 4,000m (13,000ft). Along this road lies the hut/refuge of La Joya, where an uncomfortable night's sleep is possible for those with no tent. From La Joya it takes about 3½hrs to reach the summit, 30 minutes of which is spent scrambling to the summit. The trail from the refuge to the summit is easy to find and passes through stunted forest often covered in mist. The route circumnavigates the mountain, affording occasional views, through the clouds, of the valleys below. Take care of the strong winds when crossing the ridge between the false and true summits.

Returning from the summit to Fresnito you may be tempted to cut a few kilometers off the 37km (23mi) road by using one of the numerous trails, hoping that it's a shortcut. Shauna Picard tried this and spent the best part of a day lost before finding the refuge again.

Chapter 10

Yucatán

by Jim Conrad

GENERAL INFORMATION

The Yucatán Peninsula is special because of its ancient Maya Indian ruins; Chichén Itzá, Uxmal and Tulum are the most famous, but throughout the peninsula there are literally thousands of other ruins that are seldom or never visited. The Yucatán's main roads are like tourist pipelines. At peak season it's just mind-boggling to see the numbers of tourists flooding from Cancún on daytrips down to Tulum, and the road between Mérida, on which Chichén Itzá is located, becomes reminiscent of a column of ants.

Nonetheless, once you've seen the glorious ruins, there's plenty of back-country Yucatán available for calm nature- and archeology-oriented exploration. If you can nudge yourself off the main tourist routes, the Yucatán's small towns and countryside is as pleasant and interesting as all the rest of Mexico.

CELESTÚN WILDLIFE REFUGE

Orientation

Celestún Wildlife Refuge is a 59,130ha (228sq mi) spread of land on the Gulf Coast west of Mérida; the town of Celestún is a colorful little beachside village with thatch-roofed restaurants next to the sand and some cheap hotels. Most northern tourists visit Celestún "to see the pink flamingos." More important, however, is that Celestún is considered to be the fourth most important winter migration site for birds in the entire Gulf of Mexico region.

From May to September the Carey and white turtles, in danger of extinction, nest on the refuge's beaches. Boa constrictors and crocodiles can be spotted among the mangroves. Footprints of white-tailed deer and raccoons appear around watering holes, as well as traces of jaguar and ocelot. Endemic orchids grow here, and at the river mouth lobsters, shrimp and many species of marine fish breed and grow.

If you're in a car when you cross the Río Esperanza into Celestún men rush toward you calling *"¿Flamencos? ¿Flamencos... ?"* These are boatmen eager to ferry you to isolated spots where flamingos congregate. The standard price for a flamingo trip is about US$25 per boatload; most tourists find others to go with them, to split the price.

These trips comprise a kind of acid test for whether you're a thoughtful eco-tourist, or an uninformed, insensitive snapshot-collector. Once you've paid your money and you're out there approaching the flamingos, you feel every compulsion to inch closer and closer. And all too frequently the boatmen are happy to oblige, knowing that if they do they may land better tips. Of course, the refuge's guardians try to educate the boatmen to stay a certain distance, to keep from frightening the flamingos and driving them away.

The best thing for you to do, then, before any agreement is made, is to insist that the motorboat in which you travel under no circumstance will approach the flamingos closer than the refuge's guardians permit. This will make it easier for the birds, the boatman and you. *"Ojalá que no lleguemos tan cerca a los flamencos que les molestamos... "* you can say — "I hope we don't get so close to the flamingos that we frighten them... "

The day-hike outlined here takes you along the beach, into lagoons where men collect salt much as they must have back during ancient Maya times. A kind of small, black fly is often awfully bad on this beach, so bring plenty of repellent.

Getting There

Mérida is the main large city near Celestún; Mérida's main bus station is located on Calle 69 between 70 & 72. Several buses each day depart from Mérida for Celestún, which lies 92km (57mi) to the west.

Where to Stay

Three no-star hotels in Celestún provide rooms for about US$7.50

per night; next to the beach there's a pleasant restaurant where you can sit in deep shadows beneath a thatched roof, lulled by the beach's monotonous wave-action, sipping whatever you want to sip. Usually only a handful of international travelers make it here and things stay quiet; however, on weekends visitors from Mérida liven things up. The locals say that putting a tent on the beach is OK, but you should watch out for kids who have been known to pilfer from them. Just north of town the beach becomes unpopulated and wonderfully desolate.

The Trail

You can hike north either along the beach or the one-lane, seldom-used sand road paralleling it for about 4km (2½mi), until a sand road departs to the right, heading inland. About 20 minutes of walking down this road brings you to several large, shallow ponds filled with water so saline that the salt is precipitating out. If you arrive early in the morning on a workday, you may see men collecting salt here. They wade into the ponds pulling sled-boats (usually plastic barrels cut in half lengthwise), into which wet salt from the lagoon's bottom is shoveled. Then they pull the sled-boat to shore and dump the pinkish precipitation into piles a meter high. This salt is composed of conglomerations of crystals two or three centimeters (about an inch) large; when the piles drain, the salt becomes white, and then it's collected. Apparently a prime commodity of ancient Maya commerce was salt collected here and at similar northern-Yucatán sites. Today's salt-collecting methods must be very similar to the ancient Maya's.

Though one certainly wants a picture of this time-honored activity, I feel squeamish about treating the salt-collectors as a photogenic spectacle — especially because their work is hard and couldn't possibly pay much. Many men work barefoot. They told me that sharp salt crystals cut their feet and legs and the salty water burns their cuts. Some men seem embarrassed to be seen doing such work. This situation is another test of the eco-tourist's sensibilities. I ended up not taking any pictures.

Beyond the salt-collecting ponds lie more lagoons where in the winter large flocks of white pelicans gather at dusk. Among the year-round residents of these lagoons are the brown pelican, little blue heron, American egret, reddish egret, magnificent frigate-bird, laughing gull and royal tern. In the winter several species migrate here from the north. These include the black-bellied plover, spotted sandpiper, willet, sanderling, western sandpiper, and herring gull.

On getting lost

by Hilary Bradt

It looked like a perfectly simple bit of bushwhacking; our trail had suddenly ended and the pine forests dropped sharply away. On the other side of the valley we saw patches of cultivation indicating a village nearby, and decided to descend through the trees to the road or trail that we expected to find on the valley floor. What we hadn't taken into consideration was the effect of altitude on vegetation. After about 300 metres our nice pines became a subtropical rain forest and our nightmare began. Everything was damp, furry-green and rotten. The ground gave way beneath our feet, branches we grabbed for support broke off in our hands, and many friendly looking shrubs turned out to prick or sting. It was also incredibly steep. Our descent was faster than we intended, with plants or branches that we grabbed to break our slide simply accompanying us down. "Be careful, that's a long drop!" called George helpfully as I glissaded past him hugging a loose tree. "I'm not doing this on purpose!" I said through my teeth, landing with a thump on my backpack.

The lower we dropped the denser the vegetation became until we finally reached the bottom. Relief? No, it was a river. The patches of cultivation that had tempted us down from the top were no longer in sight. All we could see was trees, trees, and more trees. And the river, which we decided to follow downstream.

We made our way down the river for several hours before camping for the night. The next morning George persuaded me that we must climb up the almost vertical canyon side since he was pretty sure he had located those cultivated milpas. We climbed. It was a repeat of the previous day, except this time we were sliding backwards. We had to grab any handhold available, relying on luck and balance when there wasn't one. As we got higher the vegetation turned into dense scrubby thorn bushes. We had to force our way through. Just as I'd reached the stage when I thought that death was preferable, we entered a clearing. A milpa!! An old one, but a definite sign of civilization. We soon found a weak trail, then an abandoned house, and finally an inhabited house with a clear trail leading up over the mountain.

Our ordeal had come to an end; it had lasted for about eight hours which was quite long enough. Looking back on the experience we realized how stupid we'd been to make the initial decision to bushwhack. When you think of the basic rules of jungle hiking, like never putting your hands or feet in places you can't see, like not taking undue risks in remote areas, we were extremely lucky. Had we been bitten by a snake, or fallen and injured ourselves, the chances of survival would have been small.

We hope readers will profit from this experience. It takes more courage to turn back than to continue on, blindly.

THE RUINS OF HORMIGUERO AND RÍO BEC

Orientation

In the Yucatán everyone visits the magnificent Maya ruins of Chichén
Itzá, Uxmal and Tulum; dozens of other sites usually stay pretty
crowded, too. Literally hundreds of ruins in the Yucatán are seldom
or never visited. This section tells how to reach two fairly impressive
(but nothing in comparison to Chichén Itzá, Uxmal or Tulum) ruins
"deep in the jungle." Hormiguero's claim to archeological fame rests
on its well preserved pyramid atop which stands a temple with a
richly ornamented door constructed to look like a monster-mouth.
Río Bec is most famous because an architectural style has been
named after it — a style in which temples are flanked by high towers
that *imitate* real pyramides. Río Bec is a large, unrestored site
spread over a wide forested area.

The town of Xpujil (also spelled Xpuhil, and pronounced shpoo-
HEEL) serves as the main jumping-off town for all the area's ruins.
This town is a good place to sit somewhere out of the way and
savor real frontier-town bustle — a steady influx of Indians hitching
into town in the backs of pickup trucks, bringing bags of corn and
beans; hard-bitten backwoods folks buying machetes and hoe
handles; young men celebrating their infrequent visit into town by
getting monstrously drunk...

Getting There

Xpujil is in southern Yucatán, on Hwy 186, between Chetumal and
Escárcega. Both first-class and second-class buses stop here. Xpujil
lies at a crossroads. The road heading north eventually reaches
Hopelchén, on the road between Campeche and Uxmal; the road
south leads to Hormiguero and Río Bec, and beyond, to truly wild
and wooly territory on the Guatemala border.

While you're around Xpujil you'll surely want to visit three fine ruins
clustered along Hwy 186. Actually, they are more spectacular than
the ruins we're telling you how to get to by hiking through the jungle.
Their only problem is that there's no hike involved in getting to them!
The ruin of Xpujil lies just 1km (⅔mi) up the hill, toward the west,
from downtown Xpujil; the ruin of Becan lies about 6km (3¾mi) west
of Xpujil, clearly visible half a kilometer off the highway, and; the ruin
of Chicaná is just 2km (1¼mi) farther west. *Taxistas* in Xpujil charge
about US$3.00 for trips to these ruins. You can camp for free beside
the parking lot at Chicaná.

Where to Stay

At this writing there are no regular lodging places in Xpujil. However, if you visit Xpujil's "touristic center of gravity," maybe something can be worked out, especially if you have a tent.

Xpujil's gravity-center is the thatch-roofed **Restaurante El Mirador Maya** atop the hill just west of town. The owner of this pleasant place, Sr Moises Carreón Cabrera, and a strayed Frenchman by the name of Serge Riou, here are at your service. By the way, guide service can be organized here, too. Serge, known hereabouts by the name of Checo, speaks passable English, as well as fluent Spanish and his native French. He takes groups no larger than five on a variety of "jungle walks" to many places far more remote than even Hormiguero and Río Bec. His current fee is about US$80 per day, per group. He prefers to walk to isolated ruins, even if they're served by dry roads that a 4 x 4 could manage. With Checo, a walking trip to the ruins of Hormiguero and Río Bec takes four days.

The Trail to Homiguero

You'll need about a day to get to Homiguero, a day to get back, and you shouldn't go without a guide unless you have fair experience in navigating, and are certain you can find your way back if you lose your direction.

Becoming disoriented on the way to Hormiguero is easy not because the ruin lies deep in the trackless jungle, but because the area is so rapidly being opened to settlement — despite the ruin lying well within the Calakmul Biosphere Reserve. In places fresh dirt roads and trails to new cornfields obliterated the main road. Only in a small area right around the ruin is the road like a tunnel through the jungle. If you don't trust your ability to navigate, but really can't afford to pay Checo to accompany you, you can hitch most of the way there, then hire a boy in the village of Ejido Castellot, which we mention below.

No bus service is available heading south from Xpuhil, so at the town's crossroads try to spot a pickup truck loading up with passengers heading south — or walk a couple of kilometers out of town, and hitch from there to avoid local traffic. At least early and late in the day there's plenty of truck traffic on this gravel road and hitching is an honored institution, so you probably won't need to wait for long.

Since most drivers on this road don't know about the ruins, you might need to specify that you want off about 14km (8.7mi) south of Xpujil, at the entrance to the village known as Ejido Castellot, which lies about 100m (100yd) off the road, on the right. Beside the road there may be a small, rusty sign announcing "Ejido: Eugenio Echeverría Castellot N° 2." After your ride most drivers expect a small *gratificación* of about US30¢.

As you hike the main dirt road heading west through Ejido Castellot, probably some boys or young men will run out offering you a guide service. Later when your path becomes obliterated because of a new cornfield, you'll be glad you hired one. If you want them to guide you to the ruin, then leave you so you can camp there overnight, you can say, "*Cuando llegamos a la ruina, usted puede regresar a su pueblo solito. Cuando regreso, no necesito a un guía*" — "When we arrive at the ruin, you can return to your village alone. When I return, I won't need a guide." If you want to try finding Hormiguero all by yourself, here's how:

Just keep walking on the dirt road heading west through Ejido Castellot. After half an hour you come to a quadrangular, 50m-long (165ft) pond on the left and probably some women washing clothes. After thirty more minutes turn right on the road that at this writing is less used than the road continuing straight. The road on which you've been walking continues southward at 200°; the grassy road to Hormiguero leads west at 290°. Now follow this grassy road through cut-over secondary woods and cornfields. After five minutes a road leads to the left, but don't take this. Try to stay on the "main road" for about 35 more minutes. If suddenly the vegetation looks more intact, that may be the ruin coming up.   As you walk along, be sure to notice those 4m wide, 0.5m high anthills! Surely this remarkable kind of ant domicile is responsible for the ruin's name, for *hormiguero* in Spanish means "anthill."

Finally arriving at the ruin, you encounter a pyramid with a monster-mouth door standing majestically "in deep jungle." The impact at the moment of finally arriving, because of the difficulty in getting there, its isolation, the ghostly ruin and the dense forest around it, rates as a premium experience.

At Hormiguero there's no office, no parking area and no cleared plaza — just rank forest and the ruins. Beneath some trees beside the main temple lies an excellent spot for camping, where you can visualize yourself lying in your tent at night, dreamily gazing through the tent's screened window, viewing the structure by moonlight. However, for the sake of security, remember that everyone who saw you between here and Ejido Castellot has been able to figure out where you were heading, and they know that this one spot beneath the trees is perfect for camping. I chose to camp at a random spot in the forest where I couldn't see anything interesting, but where no one would ever find me, except by chance.

The Trail to Río Bec

Traveling the broad gravel road between Xpuhil and Ejido Castellot, you pass the dirt-road entrance to Río Bec. When you hitch back to this entrance, probably your driver won't know its whereabouts so you may need to help him by saying that it's between the small villages of Campanario and La Lucha, heading eastward (on the left, if you're heading south from Xpujil).

The trail to Río Bec passes through forest that is much less disturbed than along the road to Hormiguero; therefore it's much more pleasant and interesting. At this writing it's impassable for 4 x 4's because a bridge is out. Though staying on the right road is a simple matter, you'd do best to have a guide lead you to the ruins. The problem is that the ruins lie a little off the road, well hidden by the forest, and you can walk right past them. Either have Checo accompany you, or hire someone in Campanario or La Lucha as a guide. If you want to stay a while at the ruin and walk back alone, returning will offer no problems.

THE RUIN OF HOCHOB

Orientation

Hochob is another Maya ruin of less interest to us for its grandeur than for the fun we have getting there. It is indeed an interesting ruin on a hill with a delightful view; but your passage through the isolated communities, farmlands and forest is what you'll remember most. Don William, described later, can outfit you with a bicycle you can ride to the ruin, and he can place you in the home of a local Indian family. Eco-tourism at its best!

Getting There

There are no real cities in the general area of Hochob; most visitors reach Hochob by turning off the road between Campeche and Uxmal, at Hopelchén, then heading southwest to Dzibalchén. From Dzibalchén you can make a somewhat rushed one-day hike to the ruins (on one of Don William's bikes it's an easy one-day trip), or you can walk it leisurely in two days.

In Hopelchén buses to Dzibalchén depart from the main plaza, in front of the store above which is written "Escalante Heredia Hnos. y Cops." The plaza itself is a shady, friendly place. About five buses a day run between Hopelchén and Dzibalchén. Probably in the future there will be more, for settlements along this road are springing up like mushrooms, which surely is bad news for the Calakmul Biosphere Reserve. Hopelchén is home to several well stocked grocery stores.

Where to Stay

In Hopelchén the hotel called **Los Arcos** lies at one of the plaza's corners, sprouting several satellite dishes on its roof. It's clean and has a restaurant; a double room with private bath, hot water and a fan on the ceiling costs about US$8.25; the **Posado Escárcega** stands at Calle 25 No. 15. Two two-star hotels are located on Avenida Justo Sierra.

Dzibalchén is a colorful, traditional, small-town base from which you can visit not only Hochob, but also the other local ruins of Dzibilnocac and Tabasqueño; a small market and some well-stocked stores can supply basic needs.

Also Dzibalchén is home to English-speaking José William Chám C., a man of Maya descent eager to provide eco-friendly services — local folks call him "Don William" (pronounced "Don Wilem"). From Don William you can rent a sturdy bike capable of surviving the bumpy gravel road to Hochob; it costs about US$3.50/ day; at this writing three bikes are available. Don William also is ready to serve as a guide himself. He won't state a standard fee but says that for a day of guiding "Americans give me about US$17.00, Germans give me US$10.00, and the Dutch about US$7.50... "

You don't really need Don William to help you find Hochob. However, if you're interested in Tabasqueño or some other secret places he knows about, he's certainly worth his pay. Possibly his most interesting service concerns providing lodging. If you find the hotel-less Dzibalchén area as pleasant as I do you may want to stay a while. Don William knows some local families willing to accept travelers into their homes.

To find Don William, stand in Dzibalchén's plaza with your back toward the Palacio Municipal. Then walk to the plaza's far left corner and continue up the street, away from the Palacio, for about 800m, until it turns hard to the left, and continue until you see a sign that says, in English, "TOURIST INFORMATION HERE." If you get lost, almost any kid in town can tell you where "Don Wilem" lives. If you'd like to set up something with him before you arrive, his address is: Sr José William Chám C./ Domicilio Conocido/ Barrio "El Pocito"/ 24920 Dzibalchén, Hopelchén, Campeche/ México.

The Trail

The seldom-traveled, one-lane gravel road from Dzibalchén to

Hochob departs from the paved Xpujil/ Hopelchén road on the northwestern side of Dzibalchén, just as you enter town, coming from Hopelchén. The intersection lies across from a cemetery, beside a huge guanacaste tree, not far from the little sign announcing Dzibalchén's outskirts; the road heads 210° to the southwest.

Eight kilometers (5mi) straight down this road lies the small town of Chincón, which is about as sleepy-looking and muddy as can be imagined. Coming into Chincón's plaza, take a hard left, pass by the small, whitewashed church and the basketball court, leave town, and pass across a field about a kilometer wide. Beyond the field, vegetation is surprisingly intact; walking the trail in early morning provides interesting birding.

Along the road between Chincón and Hochob trails sometimes depart at right angles from our road; the locals use them for collecting building poles, and to reach their beehives. Four kilometers (2½mi) from Chincón the road forks; take the arm leading to the left and stay on it. Soon you'll glimpse Hochob rising atop a hill. The plaza inside the ruin makes a wonderful picnic spot — shady and breezy, and most inviting for a mid-day snooze. It's immensely pleasant to perch on a windblown temple-foundation and gaze over the surrounding hilly landscape. Large flocks of screeching Aztec parakeets are impressive.

Three routes are available for leaving Hochob. The easiest option is to return the way you came. A second is to have the custodian, who frequently comes to the ruins from his home in Chincón, put you on the path to the ruins of Tabasqueño. Apparently, once you arrive at Tabasqueño, you can take yet another path that meets the Hopelchén/ Xpuhil road northwest of Dzibalchén. (I didn't find out about this until I was back in Dzibalchén; if you explore it, send me the details!)

The third route involves circling around toward the southeast and coming out at Dzibalchén. This is a fine walk passing through a variety of habitats, including some very pretty woods; a morning bird-walk should provide an impressive list. To take this route, return to the fork just before Hochob, turn around as if again you were coming from Chincón, and this time take the right arm instead of the left. Fifteen minutes of walking brings you to an intersection with another road, where you should take a hard left and follow the dirt road past all exits and side roads for about an hour and a half. After this period, a large path leads off to the left, to Dzibalchén. If you feel insecure taking an unmarked trail away from the main road, then just continue following the road, which eventually curves around and enters Dzibalchén.

THE RUIN OF COBÁ

Orientation

Cobá is a huge Classic Period Maya ruin (6,500 mapped structures) about 25 minutes by bus off the main road between Cancún and Chetumal. For walkers it's a dream because trails tunnel through the lush forest, interconnecting the various pyramids and temples. Maybe you'll follow a parrot around the bend and discover a Classic alter with fin hieroglyphics; climb the alter, and atop it is a meter-long, orange iguana sunning himself... At Cobá, all day long, one thing leads to another.

Though along the road between Tulum and Cobá the forest was devastated by Hurricane *Gilbert* and subsequent fires in 1985, the forest around Tulum's ruins is in good shape. Spanish moss dangles abundantly from tree limbs, and there are orchids and bromeliads, in much contrast to Chichén Itzá, which lies only 90km to the west and not much farther north. If you like using the word "jungle," then you can say that at Cobá we're at least approaching jungle conditions.

Instead of being composed of a single tight cluster of buildings, Cobá is rather a cluster of several sites linked to a central complex by long, straight causeways, or *sacbes* (wonderful walkways for nature-snooping!); more than 16 *sacbes* have been recorded at Cobá, and no one is sure why there are so many; several run through the forest for long distances only to reach what appear to be very insignificant endpoints. *Sacbe* #1 shoots from Cobá to the site of Yaxuná 100km (62mi) to the west.

Though most of Cobá is in a sorry state of preservation, two major pyramids have been excavated. One of them, Nohoch Mul, 42m (138 feet) high, is the tallest in the entire Yucatán Peninsula; from atop it you gain an impressive view of the area's lakes and forest. During Cobá's main period of influence in the 8th century, it was home to about 55,000 people, and served as an important trade center, especially for Guatemalan jade.

Getting There

On Hwy 307 between Mérida and Chetumal, the intersection with the well paved side-road to Cobá is clearly marked; it lies 1.9km (1.2mi) south of the Tulum crossroad. After traveling toward Cobá for about 24km (15mi), a well marked access road leads toward the ruins. After about 3km (1.9mi) this road ends at a small settlement with some rustic restaurants sporting signs written in English, a couple of general stores, and some curio shops with at least one advertising, in English, "The Lowest Prices in Town."

The bus from Valladolid passes the entrance to Cobá's three-kilometer-long entrance road at 0600 and 1500, heading to Playa del Carmen (thus also passing Tulum); at 0600 and 1200, buses from Playa del Carmen pass, heading for Valladolid (thus also passing the little Maya village of Punta Laguna, where you can hike looking for spider monkeys, and get to know some fine Maya folks).

Where to Stay

Visitors to Cobá can spend the night in at least four different places. The first, at the town's entrance, is a small hotel called the **Bocadito** offering rooms with private baths and ceiling fans for US$8.35 per room; on down the road, rustic lodging behind the **Restaurant Isabel** costs US$3.25 for two people. For downright elegant accommodation, turn right at the lake for **Villas Arqueológicas**, where a double room costs about US$55.00. The fourth place to spend the night is the grassy area next to the ruin's parking lot. It's free. No hook-ups.

The Trail

The idea is to be at the archeological site's entrance as early as possible — when it opens at 8AM — acquire a map, pay your entrance fee and enter, and then simply wander. You can hike all day if you wish. This is a perfect place to spot "jungle birds" or identify trees. Pointing to the amazing diversity of plants and animals here is the fact that all three species of Mexico's toucans — the keel-billed toucan, the collared araçari and the emerald toucanet — can be found here.

From atop Nohoch Mul, the big pyramid, the lakes look awfully inviting. To reach a lake, just after you enter the reserve, take the first right. Continue straight past the pyramid and follow the trail as it passes over an unreconstructed ruin and eventually descends to the water's edge. If you're lucky, here you'll discover a large tree trunk leaning horizontally above the water's surface; at *siesta* time you can lie on the trunk, cooled by friendly breezes, lulled by the sounds of waves lapping the shore beneath you, occasionally raising your binoculars to spot interesting birds in the canopy above...

The gravel road leading from the ruin's parking lot to the little Indian village across the lake should be walked at dusk and dawn by anyone interested in spotting marsh birds, or hearing the Maya language of Yucatec spoken.

Chapter 11

Chiapas

GENERAL INFORMATION

Of all the states in Mexico, Chiapas has the greatest diversity of plants and animals, as well as the most different indigenous cultures. In terms of biological and cultural affinities, Chiapas is in many respects more closely related to nextdoor Guatemala than the rest of Mexico.

About two-thirds of Chiapas's people live in rural areas — the reverse of the national ratio, and most of these people are of indigenous ancestry. The indigenous people are mosly Maya, speaking the languages of Tzotzil, Tzeltal, Tojolabal, Chol, Chontal and Lacandón. Also some non-Maya Zapotec live along the northern Pacific coast and Zoque villages are present in the Grijalva Basin.

The area around San Cristóbal is unique in Mexico in the degree that the indigenous people have maintained their culture and dignity in the face of tourism. This dignity may seem close to hostility to the camera-laden tourist who comes into their villages exhibiting blatant curiosity. The Indians simply wish to be left alone to pursue their traditional way of life without their every move being photographed.

This indifference to visitors does not extend to the inhabitants of the more remote villages and adventurous, sensitive hikers will have a rewarding time exploring other trails.

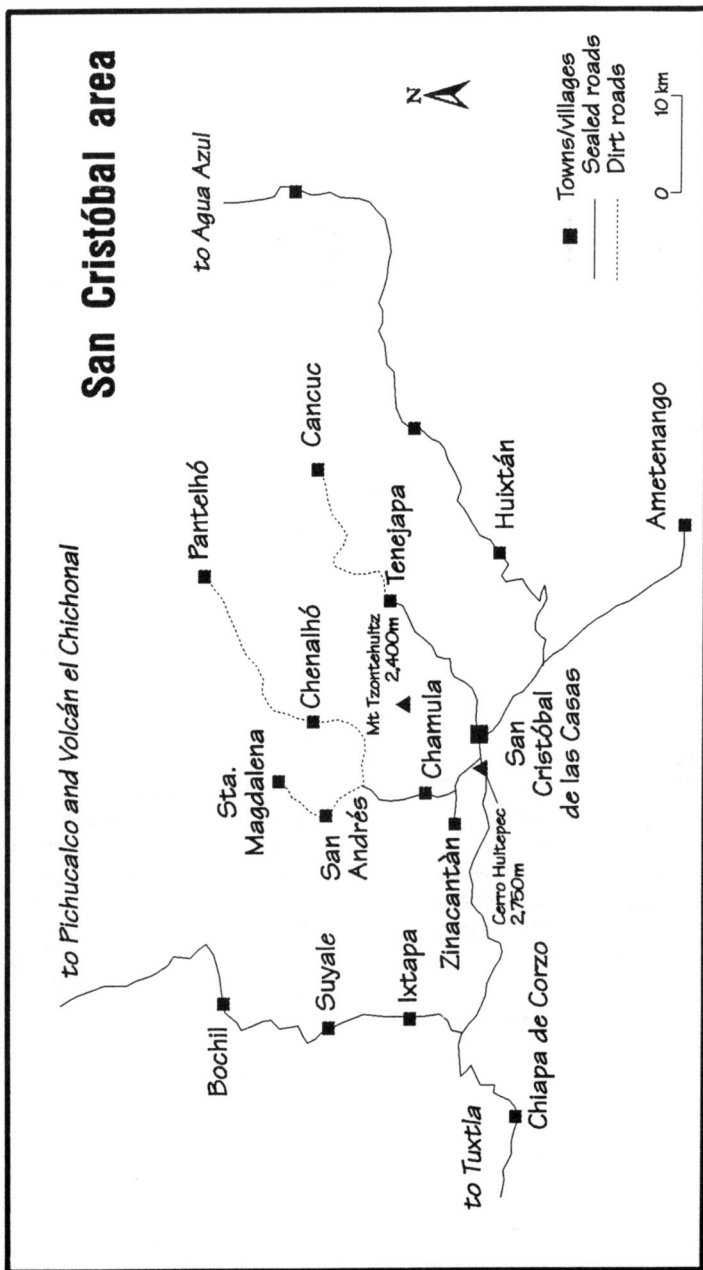

San Cristóbal area

to Pichucalco and Volcán el Chichonal

to Agua Azul

Pantelhó

Cancuc

Chenalhó

Sta. Magdalena

San Andrés

Mt Tzontehuitz 2400m

Tenejapa

Huixtán

Ametenango

Chamula

San Cristóbal de las Casas

Zinacantàn

Cerro Huitepec 2750m

Bochil

Suyale

Ixtapa

Chiapa de Corzo

to Tuxtla

N

Towns/Villages
Sealed roads
Dirt roads

0   10 km

HIKES AROUND SAN CRISTÓBAL

Orientation

San Cristóbal de las Casas is the most attractive and interesting town in Chiapas; few Mexican states are more fascinating than Chiapas. The Indians in San Cristóbal speak Tzotzil and Tzeltal, and are of Maya ancestry. Men from Zinacantán are particularly colorful with their flat, straw hats decorated with long ribbons. Chamulans are a more numerous group (their municipality covers dozens of hamlets) and wear a distinctive white woven tunic caught at the waist with a belt. Set in beautiful countryside at over 2,000m (6,500ft), the town is rightly very popular with tourists. Backpackers tend to plan a break of a day or so on their journey, but end up staying a week or more.

Getting to San Cristóbal

San Cristóbal enjoys good connections with the outside world. The first-class bus line called Cristobal Colon provides service from Mexico City's eastern terminal (the San Lázaro stop on the Observatorio/ Zaragoza Metro run).

The direct bus from Mexico City to San Cristóbal is frequently full and you must be content with a ticket to Tuxtla Gutiérrez, Chiapas's capital and largest city. Buses from Tuxtla to San Cristóbal are always crowded or even full, so in Tuxtla you may have to wait a few hours for the next empty seat. In the town of Palenque a Cristobal Colon station provides good connections.

Where to Stay in San Cristóbal

Immediately upon your arrival in San Cristóbal young men may approach you offering free information about cheap pensions and hotels; certainly they have some bargains. If you want to scout the town yourself, just step across the knee-high concrete barrier at the Cristobal Colon station, turn right onto Avenida Insurgentes, and walk north for about seven blocks until reaching the *zócalo*. For a double room the fancy **Hotel de Ciudad Real** on the *zócalo* charges about US$26.00. Four blocks away a really dingy room hardly bigger than a bed, with a communal bath, costs US$2.25. At this writing San Cristóbal has four four-star hotels, eleven three-starers, five two-starers, three that admit to being one-star, and several no-starers.

You can camp at two places in town. The most accessible is **Rancho San Nicolás** about 1km (⅔-mile) east of town at the very end of the street called Francisco León (from the *zócalo* head two blocks south, toward the Cristobal Colon station, and turn left). Here pitching a tent costs US$1.35 per person; cabañas on the hillside cost US$2.00 per person and rooms with private baths and hot water cost US$3.35. You can also here rent horses for about US$5.00 per hour, or else rent them for the whole day, from 0800 to 1500, for about US$13.75.

The other campground, more oriented toward RV's needing hookups than tent-campers (but accepting tenters), is at **Restaurante el Campestre** 3km (2mi) west of town, beyond the Periférico Pte., on the road designated as Diag. R. Larrainzar, but frequently called *la carretera a Chamula*. From the *mercado* you can take a micro-bus (*Cumbe*) to this campground; just ask for *los cumbes a San Juan Chamula*. At Restaurante el Campestre you can pitch a tent for US$1.00; with an RV it costs about US$2.70 per person, with hookups. One special attraction at Restaurante el Campestre is a steam bath.

Na Bolom

We strongly recommend a visit to the Na Bolom museum which has an exhibition of archaeological finds and a fascinating display of photos and artifacts of the Lacadon Indians, with captions in English reflecting the work done by the late Frans Blom and his wife Trudi. Señora Blom is still a figurehead at Na Bolom but a number of volunteers run the museum tours and staff the office. The hours are 10.30-12.30, 4pm-6pm. There's a small charge. Guided tours take place at 16.00.

Na Bolom also offers accommodation with 13 rooms in total of which five are in the garden at the back of the thatched hut which is reserved for Lacadonians when they come into town. Each room has been given the name of a local village and is internally decorated with paintings, tapestries and artifacts from that particular village. In addition, each room has a bath and a log fireplace for those cold evenings.

There is a price for this luxury, however. Doubles work out at around $45 a day with three meals plus an additional 10% service charge. The great thing about staying here is that guests have access to the library which has one of the largest collections of Mayan books in the world. For hikers there is a large but outdated collection of maps, some of which are Frans Blom's original drawings.

The library is also open to non-residents and is open from Tuesday to Saturday from 9am to 1pm, Monday 3pm to 6pm and is closed on Sundays. All meals are available to non-guests and are eaten in the beautiful dining room which contains a colourful tapestry which took 2,000 hours to make. Both lunch and dinner have to be booked in advance, the evening meal starting promptly at 7pm.

San Cristóbal to Chamula
by *Steven Vale*

Orientation

This makes a nice day-hike of about 4hrs. Many people ride horses along this trail. Chamula is a popular tourist destination, mostly because of its famous church. Here the Chamulans kneel on the ground, normally strewn with pine needles, next to rows of candles. On market day (Sunday) when the church is full the air smells of incense and the church's walls glow with the light of hundreds of flickering candles. In the *mercado* you can see different grades of wool being sold; mostly the stalls sell items for local trade. This is also a good place to sample *posh*, a fiery alcoholic drink made from corn (maize).

Warning   Many Chamulans dislike having photographs taken of them and it is strictly forbidden inside the church. It is rumored that two tourists were stoned to death some years ago by angry Chamulans for disregarding this rule. A confirmed murder of a tourist in the area took place in the 1950's when a German hiker had the misfortune to be climbing Mt. Tzontehuitz, a sacred mountain. If you must take photographs, then do it as discreetly as possible; I had corncobs thrown at me for taking a few general market shots. Some of the children have discovered that there is money to be made for setting up pictures; a member of our group was asked to pay to take a picture of a sheep!

The Trail

In San Cristóbal go to the municipal market on the north side of town (from the *zócalo* follow the main street, Gral. Utrilla, several blocks). Take a left onto Calle Honduras, and then turn right into Calle Argentina, which is a dirt road. After a couple of kilometers (a little over a mile) the street ends at the Periférico Norte, where you'll see some houses on the hillside above. Turn left onto the Periférico and walk about 25 minutes. At a point where the Periférico bears left, a track continues straight on. Take this and you will shortly see a stone quarry on the hillside to the right. Continue along the main track, which bears right and begins to ascend.

The dirt road, which remains wide, after a short distance passes a second stone quarry. Further on is the 1km post and thereafter a small bridge. Ignore the road branching off to the right, continue to the next bridge, and proceed up the hill. You will have been walking about 1½hr by this point and an electrical line will have become a constant companion. About 15 minutes from here another quarry, a smaller one, appears. A little further, near the 2km post, some ideal campsites appear. In July I found running water in a stream a little farther on.

The road now bears to the right (with a track branching to the left) and views of San Cristobal become available. The track levels and passes a few cornfields. Around the left bend you enter the small village of Milpoleta, which consists of a few houses situated around a small lake. Beyond the village you pass through farmland and the most beautiful section of the hike — shallow valleys interspersed with small fincas and patches of forest, numerous thatch-roofed huts, sheep grazing... Numerous trails lead both left and right.

Finally the road descends to the village of Chamula and at the cross on the left hand side it is about 1km (⅔mi) to the plaza, where the locals will probably give you a mixed reception of wariness and indifference.

Mini-buses for San Cristóbal's *mercado* depart from the plaza whenever they have a busload of passengers. The journey takes about 25 minutes and costs US30¢.

Turkish Bath

by Steven Vale

There is nothing better for aching muscles after hiking than a Turkish bath at the antiquated bathhouse of Baños Mercedarios in San Cristóbal. An hour long session costs $2 per person and for this you get your own small changing room, steam room, shower room (hot and cold) and a further room with wash basin. The steam system, which you will have to operate, takes a little getting used to. A circular tap controls the amount of steam allowed into the system and at the end of what looks like a miniature radiator is located the on/off valve. The noise is a little disturbing to start with as you get the impression that the whole thing is about to explode!

The baths are located on Primero de Marzo 55 and are open daily until 8pm except on Sunday (6pm). Take a towel and don't worry if you get thirsty. Open the main door and give a shout and the attendant can supply you with refrescos and beers.

Chamula to Zinacantán
by Steven Vale

Orientation

This hike, which takes 2 to 2½ hours, is detailed on the Bochil E15D51 1:50,000 map, a copy of which is located at San Cristóbal's Na Bolom. The Unidad Cultural de CIES at the corner of Calle Cuauhtémoc and Avenida Crescenio Rosas also has a good selection of Chiapas maps, though none for sale. I was, however, allowed to make notes. There are two INEGI offices in Tuxtla Gutiérrez (see general Mexico section for addresses).

The Trail

Take the dirt road west out of Chamula as far as the main road. Cross the highway and continue straight for about 2km (1¼mi) to where the dirt road passes a couple of shops as it proceeds uphill. Further up the hill is a crossroads, with a cross on the right and, on the left, a path to what is apparently a deserted school. Follow this track, ignoring any side trails, which winds its way along the hilltops, eventually affording excellent views of Zinacantán and its church. Eventually the path descends steeply to the main road. (Note that photography is forbidden in the churches of this region.)

Cerro de Moxviquil
by Steven Vale

Orientation

There's not really much to this 3-4hr, sometimes rather steep hike. I've included it because travelers in San Cristóbal who stay longer than planned often run out of places to go. This hike takes you in a circle through countryside with lots of butterflies and hummingbirds. Somewhere on Cerro de Moxviquil Maya ruins were excavated by Frans Blom more than 30 years ago; artifacts from the site are on display at Na Bolom. However, now the site is overgrown and the ruins are not at all apparent.

The Trail

Walk out of town along Avenida Yajalón, which is reached by either Avenida Comitán or Avenida Cristóbal Colón. You'll pass a tortillaría and eventually reach a spot where on the left there's an old brick-

San Cristóbal - Chamula - Zinacantan hike

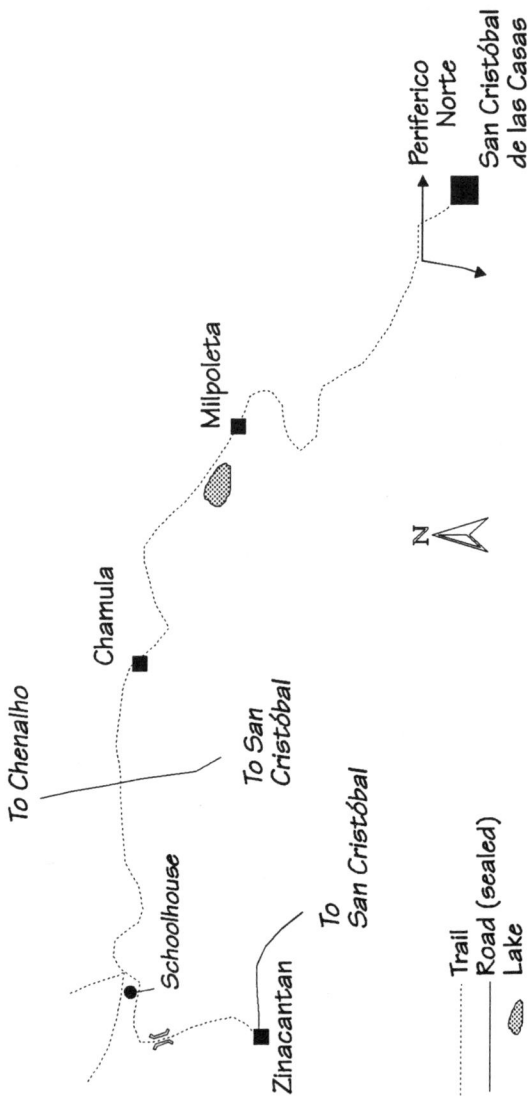

To Chenalho

Chamula

Schoolhouse

Zinacantan

To San Cristóbal

To San Cristóbal

Milpoleta

Periferico Norte

San Cristóbal de las Casas

N

Trail
Road (sealed)
Lake

making business in a grassy area, and on the right there's the Río Amarillo. An old building (a mill) with pillars can be seen on the left after crossing the small bridge.

Continue to the Periférico and straight on along the dirt road that passes between a number of houses before ending at the local outdoor washing facilities, or *ojo de agua*. Here the single track passes to the right of the water, climbs a few meters and splits. Take the right and climb steeply past a couple of huts. Here you may be asked to pay US20¢ each for use of the trail. This is commonplace on many trails around San Cristobal; payment is optional.

A steady stream of Indians use the trail, which eventually passes an adobe house selling bottled drinks. A few minutes farther up the hill the trail forks again at a series of rock steps. Could these be the ruins? From here on there are routes to both Chamula and Pozuelos; many villagers use these trails so ask a local for directions. You can also make circular routes on the hilltop and return by one of the descending trails which will take you back to San Cristóbal (again, ask a local person to confirm that you are heading in the right direction.

If this vagueness makes you anxious, ask one of the volunteers at Na Bolom for directions to the ruins. They are familiar with the area.

Hiking in the Tenejapa area
by Steven Vale

Tenejapa lies in a beautiful valley at an altitude of 2020m and is a good starting/finishing point for a number of hikes.

Half day hike

This easy hike follows a trail which climbs out of Tenejapa where it eventually rejoins the road to San Cristóbal. Leave the plaza from the far left corner when standing with your back to the church. A dirt road leads between the houses and forks right, where a single track continues straight on up into the trees. It is a steep path and will be slippery if it has been raining. After 15 minutes the first clearing is reached after which the trail narrows and is hemmed in by huge ferns. Further up the hill to the left is another flat grass clearing where the trail widens. Hikers wishing to get an early start on other trails in the area will find good campsites at the end of a further trail which branches off to the right after about 50m.

The main trail keeps the Tenejapa Valley to the right and soon narrows where you might come across locals collecting firewood. At the fork, take the left branch which climbs into a section of pine

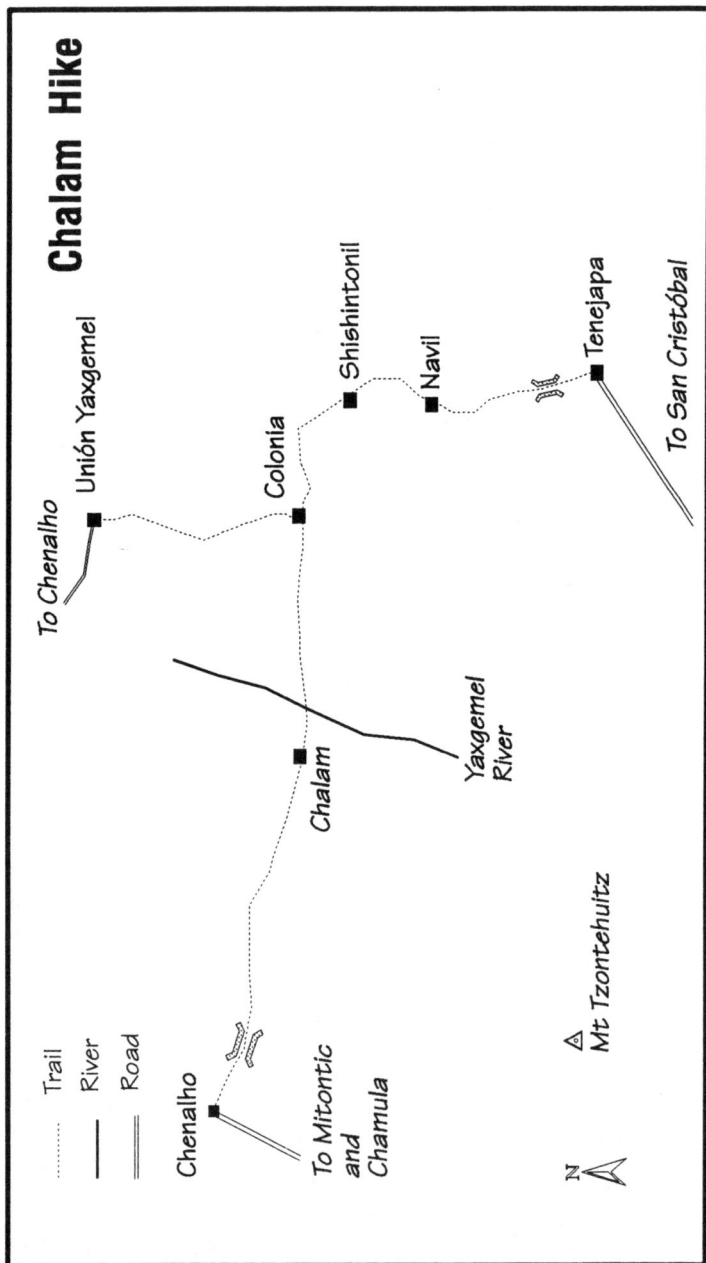

Chalam Hike

Trail
River
Road

To Chenalho

Unión Yaxgemel

Colonia

Shishintonil

Navil

Tenejapa

To San Cristóbal

Yaxgemel River

Chalam

Chenalho

To Mitontic and Chamula

Mt Tzontehuitz

N

forest. The path is at times quite steep and after a kilometer arrives at a section of oak forest before ending at a dirt road. It is supposed to be possible to gain access to Cerro Tzontehuitz by turning right on the dirt road. The left side returns to the main Tenejapa/San Cristóbal road reaching it in about 600m at the km23 post. From here it is east to stop a passing Combi or enjoy the landscape with a stroll along the road towards San Cristóbal where numerous short cuts pass through both meadows and forested land.

Tenejapa to Chalam hike
by Steven Vale

This is a long day hike starting from Tenejapa and passing through several *communidads* where gringos are rarely seen. For the most part the trail is faint and passes through sections of dense cloud forest, cleared areas utilised by milpas, and provides superb views of the valley before the trail descends steeply into the village of Chalam.

Directions

From standing in the plaza with your back to the church take the far right hand road which continues out of town with the trail up the hillside clearly visible to the left. This is reached by taking a left shortly before reaching what looks to be an artificial mound. Here, the dirt road passes between a group of houses and ends at the hillside where a path continues to the left though a further trail heads up the steep hillside. The trail is frequented (particularly on market day) by a steady stream of villagers, so if in any doubt ask for the path to Navil.

Do not let the initial steep ascent put you off as it flattens out after 1-1½ hours at a number of limestone boulders. Fortunately, the first stage demands plenty of pauses as there are fine views of Tenejapa/ On the flat path above we met some Navil villages who could not believe that we were trying to reach Chalam. Their estimated arrival time varied from 5 hours to 3 days and further along the trail we were told that no path existed.

Continuing, the track soon starts to descend through corn fields and after a further hour look for a hut on the left displaying both Fanta and Coca Cola signs. Shortly afterwards the trail forks (the first of many). Take the left side which descends to the Navil schoolhouse. Keep this on your right and head towards a number of buildings on the hilltop (the first of these is the church). At the next fork a path heads uphill to these buildings though keep on the main trail which turns to the right (keeping the church out of sight and to the left). On the other side of the hill the trail descends with more milpas on the left; on the furthest one stands a hut with a Coca Cola sign. The friendly owner provided us with tiny chairs as he scratched directions in the soil to the next village — pronounced as Shishaltontic. Allow 2½-3 hours to this point.

The main track continues through deforested areas, and piles of limestone blocks protrude through dense regrowth. Some 30 minutes after leaving the Coca Cola hut the trail descends steeply and two thatched abodes can be seen on the hill in front. On the next ascent the trail forks shortly before the treeline. Take the left branch and continue into the pine forest. Continue climbing and after a further undulating section the path forks again. Take the right side which leads into the corn fields and at the following fork, again turn right, which keeps corn fields to the left.

After a further mostly downhill section through pine trees, the trail again provides views of two thatched huts. At the next fork take the left side as the right leads to the huts. Continuing along the main trail a series of stone steps provide views over the *communidad* of Shishintonil. Follow the path to the right keeping the village to the left and after a short distance the trail arrives (literally) on the basketball court.

The trail continues on the other side of the basketball court and arrives at a thatched shelter (left) with a three-ways fork ahead. Take the left path which leads steeply downhill and at the following fork head right, which eventually provides views over a small valley, with thatched huts on the far hillside and what looks to be a set of ruins further to the right. Descend into the valley and at the bottom take the right fork. This cuts through the tall cornfields crossing the hill somewhere between the huts and the possible ruins.

After leaving the cornfields the path continues uphill and the next fork is easily missed. Look for the faint trail which continues into the cloud forest (there are good views to the right). The left, more distinct trail leads to three huts guarded by some 15 aggressive dogs. The trail continues through the forest and at the next clearing (cornfield) fork left. At the next fork keep to the right and head back into the forest. The muddy path arrives at a grass clearing. Keep left and the trail heads down through the bushes to a further small clearing. In the opposite corner a steep path cut into the rock leads straight up the hill which eventually levels and continues through dense cloud forest. In a short while views open up over a broad valley and a village can be seen down to the right. If it has been raining the descent trail will be terrible and although we took a trail leading to the village there are apparently trails heading off to the left providing a quicker route to Chalam. By taking a right fork every time on the descent, the path quickly descends to a dirt road. Turn left here and walk about 1½km in the direction of Colonia. On the way the road passes a school (right) and eventually ends at a steep uphill section leading to a basketball court. Here, the locals crowded around to look at our maps and at about the same time a bus arrived.

There is one daily service to San Cristóbal, via Tenejapa, which departs from the basketball court at 4am sharp every morning. Here, the hiker is faced with several options. It is possible to return in the bus the following morning; hike 3 or 4 hours to the village of Union Yaxgemel on the far side of the valley where collectivos make the 1½ to 2 hour trip to Chenhalo, or hike to Chalam from where there is a day hike to Chenhalo.

To get to Chalam, a dirt road branches off to the left about 100m before reaching the basketball area. The journey takes 1 to 1½ hours and in places the road has been washed away or blocked by mudslides. There are no cars here and the only form of transport is the daily bus service.

Variations

We took the 4am bus from Colonia back to San Cristóbal, a journey time of 2½ hours, though it is possible to continue on to the villages of Chenhalo and Mitontic. Chenhalo is reached by continuing into Chalam and out on a trail at the opposite end of the village which heads uphill to the ridge. It is easy to ask directions from here and you may even find someone willing to act as a guide in Chalam. From the final ridge there are good views over the valley and the village of Chenalho which is reached via a steep downhill path. The village lies at 1500m, and has been home for the past 25 years of a French priest — Padre Miguel Chanteau. On another visit we were given a guided tour by him which included the church, a short hike to the temple, in addition to sampling chi-chi beer (made from crushed sugar cane). The padre also has a number of bunkbeds for those wishing to stay overnight and can arrange meals for around $2 each. Mitontic can also be reached in a day from Chalam. Ask at the village for directions.

Practical information

Conditions/What to bring   At least one overnight is unavoidable so a sleeping bag is essential. There are a few suitable camping areas on the hilltop before descending into Chalam, and for those without a tent it is possible to ask around and find shelter for the night. There is little water en route though in the early stages bottled drinks can be bought. In the wet summer months pack a set of dry clothes into plastic bags. If you can survive on a few tortillas and a cup of coffee fine — otherwise take your own food. A flashlight is essential for the early morning walk to the bus from Chalam.

Height Gain   From Tenejapa the gain is little more than 300m with gradual ascents/descents during the day before arriving at Chalam at 1700m.

Maps   The Oxchuc E15D52 1:50,000 map (DETENAL) 1984 edition is useful for village names though does not list all the trails.

Footnote   Asking directions from villagers is difficult and distances are almost always incorrect. Some locals refer to Chalam as Chenalho, simply because Chalam is in the so-called state of Chenhalo. The same is true of Navil which is in the state of Tenejapa. The occupants of remote *communidads* refer to Tenejapa as Ciudad Tenejapa!
   In this culturally sensitive area you should leave your camera at home and ask permission before crossing what may be private land.

Getting there   Tenejapa is about an hour by collectivo, the first one leaving the market area at 7am. If starting from Chenhalo it is easier to take a collectivo to the Chamula turnoff and simply wait for a passing truck for the 1 to 1½ hour trip.

The Nature Trail in PRONATURA's Ecological Reserve (the Ox Yoquet trail)
by Jim Conrad and Steven Vale

PRONATURA is Mexico's most successful environmental organization. Its Reserva Ecológica PRONATURA, about 1.5km (1mi) west of San Cristóbal, on the road to San Juan Chamula, represents part of its effort to inform people about, and to preserve, Mexico's natural history. A 2km (1¼mi) interpretive trail passes through the reserve, which covers a slope of Cerro de Huitepec. The Tzotziles call this extinct volcano Muktavitz, which translates into great mountain. It is said to be nearly 1 million years old. Another name is Ox Yoquet (Maya Tzotzil). Ox means three, and Yoquet peaks which, traditionally, translates into the three rocks where the tortilla cooking and heating grill (*comal*) rests. Signs in Spanish explain things. At the entrance posters, cards and guides to the trail can be purchased. There is no set admission charge, though donations are appreciated and needed. Opening times seem to vary, and

PRONATURA

by Steven Vale

This Mexican conservation organisation has its headquarters in Mexico City (see *Addresses*). In Chiapas PRONATURA has an office in San Cristóbal at Josefa Ortiz de Dominguez No 27A though there are rumors of a move to Real de Mexicanos No 10 (close to the Santo Domingo church). The offices of ECOSFERA (Center for Studies in the Conservation of Natural Resources) can be found in the same building.

All the staff speak English and vice-president Ignacio March (known as Nacho) is particularly knowledgeable on good hiking areas particularly in the Lacadonian jungle where he has been on long scientific expeditions. PRONATURA is supported by a number of international organizations including World Wide Fund for Nature, Wildlife Conservation International, American Museum of Natural History and the University of California which is currently working on producing a set of cartographical maps which should be available for sale soon.

The Chiapas office is a good place to gain further information on Montez Azules (Lacadonian Forest), Selva de Octote caves, La Venta Canyon, Calacmul and Sian Ka'an where crocodiles can be seen.

ADDRESSES

PRONATURA head office is based in Mexico City at Avenida Nuevo Leon No 144, Col. Hipodromo Condesa. C.P. 06100 (Tel: 91 (5) 2-86-96-42). Lorenzo Sada is a good contact here for information on the Reserva Mariposa Monarco (Monarch Butterfly Reserve) in the Uruapan area.

Joanne Andrews is the director of PRONATURA in the Yucatán and works with four major peninsula parks. Joanne can be contacted at Calle 13 No 203A, Col. Garcia Gineres, Merida, Yucatán (Tel: (99) 25-10-04).

Director Juan Bezaury of Amigos de Sian Ka'an A.C. (Friends of Sian Ka'an) can be contacted at Plaza America, 2nd Floor, Locales 48-50, which is on the corner of Avenida Coba, between Nube and Lluvia, in Cancum, Quintana Roo (Tel: (988) 4-22-01).

Details of the newly opened Triumfo Biosphere Reserve which covers a large area along the top of the Sierra Madre del Sur can be obtained from Victor Hugo at Tuxtla Zoo where an office supplying maps and permits can be found. Again there is no set charge though donations are welcomed.

sometimes the gate is closed, even when the reserve is supposed to be open, so you might want to give them a call at 8-06-97 before making a visit. Officially the hours are 9am to 6pm daily.

Oak trees predominate in the reserve and a fine assortment of

Lagunas de Montebello

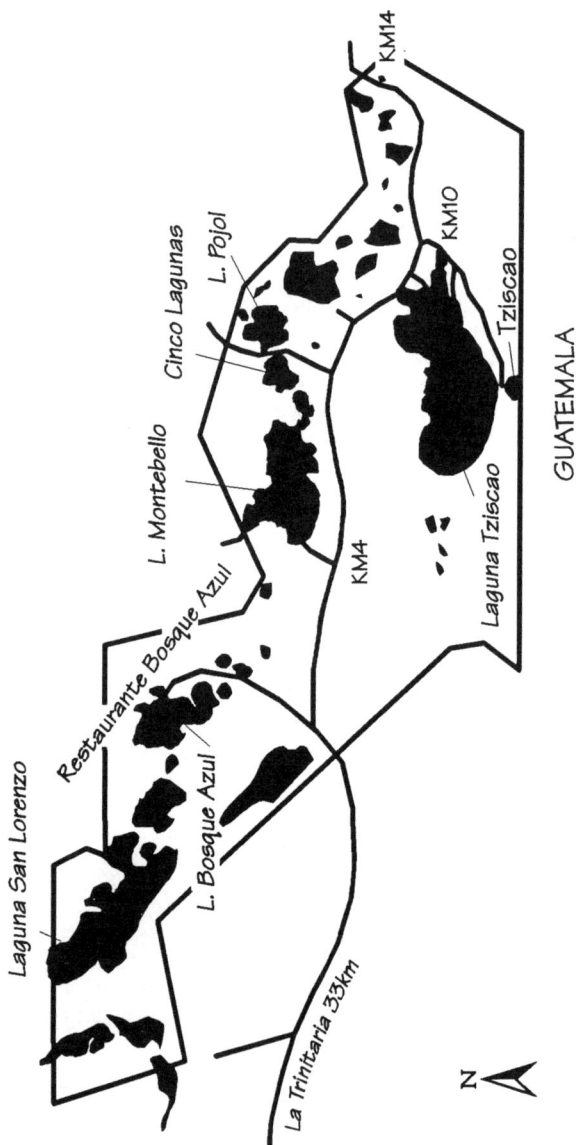

KM14

KM10

Tziscao

GUATEMALA

L. Pojol

Cinco Lagunas

L. Montebello

KM4

Laguna Tziscao

Restaurante Bosque Azul

L. Bosque Azul

Laguna San Lorenzo

La Trinitaria 33km

N

birds can be spotted here. For example, among the "exotics" are the mountain trogon, blue-throated motmot, brown-backed solitaire, ruddy-capped nightingale-thrush and green violet-ear. Most of the reserve's mammals are nocturnal, so probably you won't see many. However, the diurnal Chiapas gray squirrel frequently is seen among the oaks, and sometimes you can spook up the Chiapan race of the cottontail rabbit; other species that are more strictly nocturnal include the *tlacuache* (opossum) comadreja (weasel), and various species of *musaraña* (shrews) and *roedores* (mice and rats).

The cloud forest section contains bromelids, which are epyphitic plants, living on trees without harming them. They have bright red flowers. There are a number of rain shelters on the trail, though bring good waterproof gear during the wet season.

Getting There

The reserve stands at Km 3.5 on the road to Chamula. You can walk there in a little over an hour, striking west from the *zócalo* on Diego de Mazariegos, and continuing west on *la carretera a Chamula*; however, it's not a particularly pleasant walk. The easiest and most colorful route is to go to the mini-bus area of the *mercado* on the northern end of Gral. Utrilla and take a *cumbe* toward Chamula or Zinacantán, getting out at *la reserva*.

LAGUNAS DE MONTEBELLO NATIONAL PARK
by Jim Conrad

Orientation

Here you find high-elevation, cool, good-smelling pine forests. This is a big park, covering 6,022ha (23sq mi) holding 68 lakes inter-connected by footpaths... You can really let your hair down and stay for a while. Small boys greet new arrivals as they step from *cumbes* upon arrival, asking to serve as guides to *las grutas*. The *grutas* are a couple of natural bridges not 1km away. Though they're easy to find by asking directions at every corner, to get there you must pass across ground that feels like other peoples' private back yards, and go through at least one gate that seems to have been placed there to keep people out; paying a boy to go with you is worth the money, if only to keep from feeling like an intruder. The boys steadfastly refuse to quote a price for their services, but I saw them walk away looking disgusted at a fellow traveler's offer of US35¢.

It's astonishing how you can leave Comitán or even La Trinitaria on a hot, sunny day with hardly a cloud in the sky, but arrive at the park — without changing elevation or crossing hills — in a cold drizzle, even during the dry season. Therefore, any trip to the park should begin with rain gear and warm clothing near at hand, no matter how absurd it seems at the trip's beginning. Nights in the park can be downright cold.

Getting There

In Comitán, micro-buses leave every hour or so throughout the day for Montebello from the offices of Transportes Lagos de Montebello at 3ª Norte, Poniente. A one-way ticket from Comitán all the way to the park — a distance of about 58km (36mi) — costs approximately US$1.20.

If you're coming from San Cristóbal or Guatemala, there's really no need to enter Comitán unless you want to stock up on food. If you're traveling by bus on Hwy 190, buy a ticket to La Trinitaria, which lies 16km (10mi) southeast of Comitán, and ask to be let off at "*la entrada de Lagunas de Montebello*" — the entrance to Lagunas de Montebello. This access road lies on the Comitán side of La Trinitaria. Once you're deposited at the intersection, a *cumbe* from Comitán will probably come within an hour; it costs about 80¢ for the 42km (26mi) to the park.

Where to Stay

The park's "touristic heart" is **Restaurante Bosque Azul**, lying right below the turnaround at the end of the *cumbe* route. Here the owner, María del Carmen al Boris, will provide such services as sell you food, direct you toward horse and boat rentals, help you get a guide, and show you where to camp in a grassy area below the restaurant, right at the lake's edge, next to a workable toilet. Doña María refuses to establish a set price for her services. "*No es caro, es barato,*" is all she'll go on record saying. A visitor told me that US$3.30 per hour for horseback riding was about right.

CASCADES OF AGUA AZUL
by Jim Conrad

Orientation

Along the main road across the Chiapas highlands, between San Cristóbal and Palenque, Agua Azul's cascades are truly cascades, not high waterfalls; nor are they particularly rambunctious cascades. However, that's one of the nice things about them. They're spectacular enough to be interesting, yet small and friendly enough to play with. Swim, wade, sit near them and read... When the sunshine mingles with their sparkling bluish waters (*agua azul* means blue water), it's irresistibly inviting. The most spectacular fall lies about 4km (2½mi) below camp, accessible by a trail along the river.

Getting there

Walk into any travel agency in Palenque or San Cristóbal and they'll have ways to get you there in fancy buses at fancy prices. However, do-it-yourself travelers can get there more cheaply. In Palenque, at the Chambalo *cumbe* service, at 10am and 1pm *cumbes* leave for Agua Azul, costing about US$5.00 per person. Even cheaper are the regular buses running between San Cristóbal and Palenque, which stop at Agua Azul; tickets on them cost about a dollar. The cascades lie about 62km (36mi) south of Palenque.

Since the trip from Palenque takes only about 1½ hours, on a regular bus it's possible to leave Palenque early in the morning, spend the day at Agua Azul, and return the same day. Palenque's *cumbes* carry their passengers all the way to the falls, but if you arrive on a regular bus you'll be deposited about 4km (2½mi) short of your destination. The walk from the bus stop to the falls is entirely, and steeply, downhill; it takes about an hour to walk.

Where to Stay

No hotels operate in Agua Azul at this time, but camping is excellent both for tenters and RVers (no hook-ups). The ticket to enter the area in a car costs US$1.65; by foot about 65¢. Camping costs US$1.65 per person, and renting a hammock slung in a *palapa* costs the same, though if you want a mosquito net over your hammock it costs about US$3.35. Horses can be rented, but expect to negotiate. Two restaurants are available and most of the time local folks circulate peddling bananas and other fruits.

Volcán el Chichonal hike

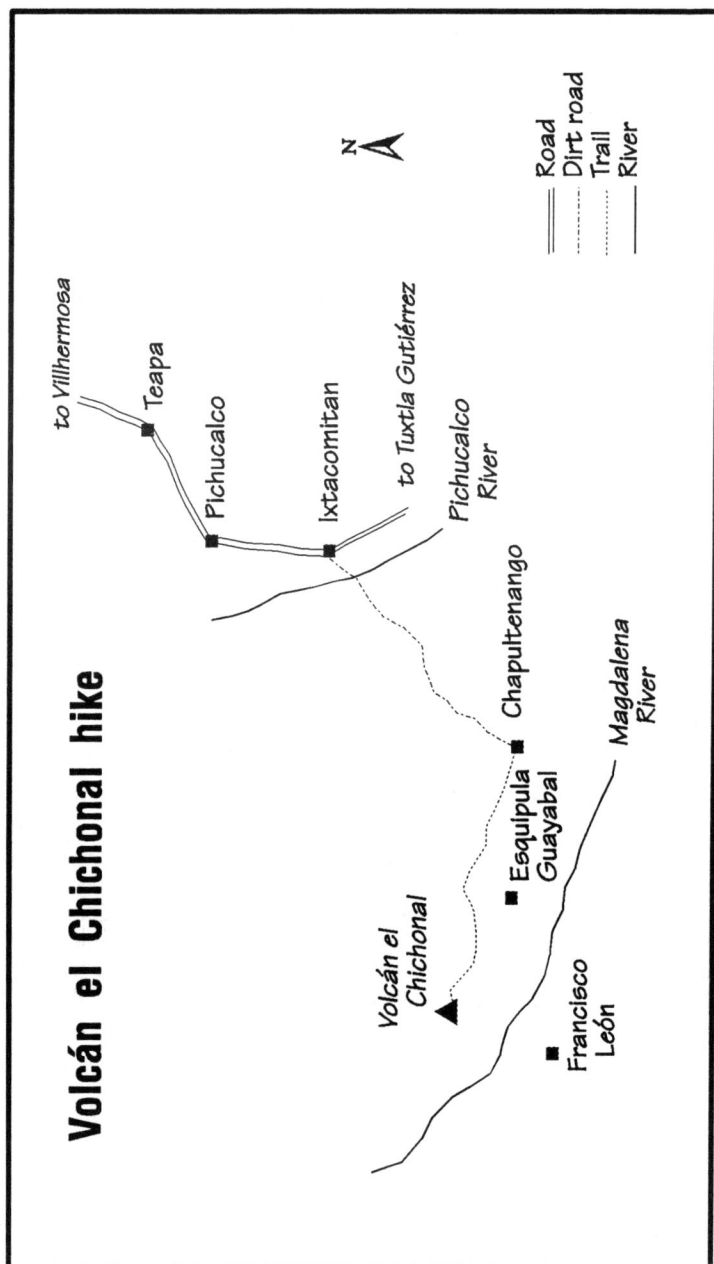

VOLCÁN DE EL CHICHONAL
by Steven Vale

Orientation

Here we describe two ways to get to El Chichonal — one involving hiring a guide and horses, and the other, which only experienced hikers and good map-readers should attempt, going without a guide.

El Chichonal, also known as El Chichón, created international headlines during March and April of 1982 when it erupted, spewing death and destruction to numerous villages in the area. Ash was deposited as far away as the ruins of Palenque and San Cristóbal, and a volcanic cloud encircled the earth, probably affecting the world's climates in ways not yet understood.

Fortunately, many of the surrounding villages were evacuated in time. However, when people returned there was no trace to be found of the villages of Francisco León, Nicapa, Chapultenango, Esquipula Guayabal, El Naranjo and the village of El Chichón itself. Even the Río Magdalena's course was changed.

Situated in the remote northwest of Chiapas, the nearest major cities are Villahermosa and Tuxtla Gutiérrez. Due to its relative inaccessibility, at least 3 days are required for this trip. Because the volcano has again slipped into obscurity, you are unlikely to meet any other *gringos*; occasionally Mexican tourists make the journey with 4 X 4's. Although still potentially active, there have been no further eruptions since 1982. Nonetheless, the crater is far from dormant.

Permanent steam columns rise from large pools in the 100m deep (330ft) crater. Nowadays the scene is quiet, though the yellowish green color produced when sulphur from the steam vents mixes with oxygen is plainly visible. Chichonal's eruption reduced its height of 1,260m (4,135ft) by 200m (656ft); the dome was simply blown away. This has created an inner crater inside the remains of an outer one, which resulted from an ancient eruption. From the crumbling lip of the inner crater, views of steaming pools can be observed.

Getting There

From either Villahermosa and Tuxtla go to Ixtacomitán, on Hwy 195, about 12km (7½) south of Pichucalco. First-class buses depart from Villahermosa for the 2 hour journey at 7am, 10:30am, 3pm, 9pm, 10pm and 11pm. If planning an overnight stop in the area, there are four lodging places in Pichucalco, but none in Ixtacomitán; there are a number of restaurants in Ixtacomitán, however.

From Ixtacomitán it is necessary to take a two-hour ride in a truck to the village of Chapultenango. The departure point is shortly before entering Ixtacomitán from Villahermosa, where the road turns a sharp left and leads uphill. On the bend a sign for Chapultenango points to the dirt road on the right; if you miss it, it's only a 10-minute walk back downhill from the plaza.

Follow the dirt road a few hundred meters past a couple of cattle pens, to a store on the right. The first truck departs from here at noon. Thereafter trucks are rumored to leave at 1 and 2pm though the noon truck eventually left at 1:30pm with no sign of the 1pm departure.

The noon truck arrives in Chapultenango early enough to organize a guide and horses for the following morning. On arrival ask for Enrique Reyez at Posada El Mico, who does the arranging; the best guide is reported to be Enrique Mejía. Expect to pay about $10 for a guide and $5 for each horse. Enrique Reyez will also arrange lodging in Chapultenango for about $2 each. Food is available at Lucía's, a sort of restaurant. The trip in follows parts of the original dirt road that lead to the destroyed village of Volcán Chichonal.

Once your hike is over and you're back in Chapultenango, your only way of getting back to Ixtacomitán, apart from walking, is to take one of three regular trucks which depart at 4, 5 and 6am. In Ixtacomitán second class buses leave from the plaza to Pichucalco; you may have to wait a while to get a place in a Tuxtla-bound bus.

Going Without a Guide

Experienced hikers may wish to find their own route to the volcano, and possibly then head farther southwest to the village of Francisco León, which suffered the greatest damage of all the area's populations. Here the wall of lava and ash was so powerful that it dammed the Magdalena River, creating an artificial lake; the river now follows a different course.

The INEGI office in Mexico City puts out a 1:50,000 map of the Ixhuatán area, covering the area in which we're interested. As with many Mexican maps, it unfortunately uses a satellite photograph taken in 1972 before the eruption, so much of the information is unreliable. Of particular interest to hikers planning their own route is that the road through Tectuapán and Nicapa no longer exists. Other problems are those of water availability. Many of the marked streams have been rerouted and others no longer exist. Another map, also outdated, is the 1:250,000 Villahermosa E15-8. A copy of this exists in the library at Na Bolom, in San Cristóbal.

PALENQUE RUINS TO NARANJO VILLAGE
by Jim Conrad

Orientation

Originating inside the ruins of Palenque (you must first buy a ticket to the ruin), this trail crosses a high hill, and after 6km (4mi) reaches the town of Naranjo. Sometimes howler monkeys can be heard along the way. Early in the morning it's an excellent bird-walk. A small river at the end makes a great picnic and cooling-off spot.

The first part of this trail climbs quite steeply for a surprisingly long while; when it's wet, the stones become dangerously slick. However, during the climb several spots provide excellent views into surrounding treetops, so you can catch your breath and add species to your bird list at the same time. The trail is heavily used by Indians who often will be happy to talk your leg off.

Getting There

The town of Palenque is accessible by buses, most coming either from San Cristóbal and Agua Azul in the south, or from the city of Villahermosa in the north. In Villahermosa the first-class ADO buses to Palenque often are full. If this happens to you, just walk a few blocks to the second-class bus station (ask, *¿Donde está el terminal de autobuses de segunda clase, por favor?*) and take buses that carry you part of the way, if not all the way.

Connections between the town of Palenque and the ruins are excellent. About every ten minutes throughout the day, *cumbes* travel between them, leaving from two places on Calle Allende; one-way passage costs about US33¢.

Where to Stay

The town of Palenque is full of hotels; it's a major tourist destination, and the tourist office will supply you with armloads of literature listing places to stay. The **Maya Bell**, a campground located between town and the ruins, deserves special mention because for about US$1.35 a day you can pitch a tent here. Having no tent, you can negotiate for a rented hammock to hang inside a thatched-roof palapa. Maya Bell even has showers and toilets. Sometimes here at dawn and dusk you can hear howler monkeys roaring in the distance. To get to Maya Bell, when you take a *cumbe* from town, just say to the driver "Maya Bell," and he'll know exactly where you're going.

The Trail

Locate the Temple of Inscriptions, the main pyramid at Palenque — the one everyone climbs and then descends into the funerary crypt to see the magnificent stone sarcophagus lid. On the Temple's left side you should see steep stone steps leading up the densely forested hill. Climb these steps and on the well-worn dirt trail leading away from the plaza area and the temple continue ascending the hill, keeping parallel with the small stream on your left. About 50m (50yd) up the path you'll pass by a small temple with a good view of the stream. Six kilometers (4mi) later, you'll come to a stream called the Río Chacamás and the small settlement of Adolfo López Mateo. Ford the stream and soon you'll reach the town of Naranjo, which is large enough to support a store.

BONAMPAK

by Jim Conrad

Orientation

Bonampak is a favorite destination for ruin-visitors who can afford to fly there, or else endure the strenuous overland trip; this is the "ruin deep in the jungle" par excellence. People mainly want to see "the Bonampak murals" — well preserved paintings on the walls of one of the structures. The murals, dated soon after 800 AD, narrate the story of a battle, its aftermath, and the victory celebrations afterwards.

Getting There

The town of Palenque is the main starting point for people going overland. At this time, anyone visiting the ruins by land will need to endure ample bumps, mud and/ or dust, and a walk through the rain forest. During the rainy season the approximately 160km (100mi) gravel road between Palenque and Bonampak is, in many places, an absolute quagmire. During the dry season a few challenging spots remain, though a 4 X 4 should have few problems, other than for the interminable bumps and dust. During the dry season a bus needs 7½ hours from Palenque to the access road leading to Bonampak; *cumbes* and 4 X 4s need four or five, depending on how fast the driver is willing to hit bumps.

With the *cumbe* cooperative on Palenque's Calle Allende between Avenida Miguel Hidalgo and Avenida Juárez you can make a one-day trip to Bonampak (up early, a lot of hard, bumpy riding, and home late); the cost depends on how many people go. The cooperative expects approximately US$200 to make the trip; if you go with six other people, then, it costs about US$30.00. Even if you're not a member of a party of six and want to go, you can usually find a travel agency with a handwritten sign on its door reading something like, "We need two more passengers for Bonampak tomorrow." The cooperative also offers two-day trips, which include a voyage down the Usumacinta to the ruin of Yaxchilán. All food and sleeping arrangements are taken care of; this costs about US$85.00 per person, as long as at least five people go. These prices vary a little, depending on lots of things, not the least of which are road conditions.

Even if you go in a *cumbe* or a tourist bus you'll still have to walk about 10km (6mi) along a trail that, in places, can be inordinately muddy. During the wet season when *chiclero* horses packing out chicle chop up the trail the mud becomes knee-deep and can suck off boots and socks. The best I have ever seen the trail was in early March, well into the dry season, when mud in the worst places was still ankle deep.

It's possible to get to Bonampak for even less than the cost of a *cumbe* ticket; my last visit cost US$8.00, round-trip from Palenque. This was by using the second-class bus-line called "Linea de Pasajeros Comitán Lagos de Montebello" on Avenida Manuel Velasco S. about three blocks west of the *mercado*. Here's how that works:

Since Bonampak is in a frontier region into which services are being expanded gradually, erratically and painfully, bus schedules change frequently. Thus the day before you plan to leave for Bonampak you should visit the bus office, note the posted schedule, and verbally confirm that on the next day they do indeed intend to leave at the posted time. At this writing, the "Bonampak bus" is the one leaving at 0900 for Frontera Corozal, also known as Echeverría. After about 7½ hours of being shaken quite adequately you'll be deposited at an intersection about 15km (9mi) from Bonampak, next to a small community of Lacandón Indians.

Where to Stay

Between Palenque and the ruins there are no regular lodging places. Either you must try to reach the ruins before nightfall or camp.

Tenters might negotiate a price for pegging a tent in the yard of a Lacandón Indian at the entrance to the town of Bethel, which stands about 500m before you come to the Bonampak trail head; the individuals in the first two huts next to the road are quite accustomed to renting parking spaces and other forms of dealing with the public. However, don't go wandering through the rest of the village.

Once you reach Bonampak you can peg a tent in an extensive grassy area or even sleep in a bunkhouse beneath mosquito netting. The custodians won't say what an appropriate *gratificación*, or tip, might be for providing such luxury. The custodians and their families will even provide meals and guide service, and they'll insist that there's no set price for anything, but clearly in this isolated spot where everything must be carried in and the people live in such seclusion, generous *gratificaciones* are particularly appropriate.

The Trail

From the intersection where the bus lets you off, on the main road between Palenque and Frontera Corozal, walk in a generally southwest direction for about an hour — 4km (2½mi). When the road bends to the right, and on the left a footpath leads into the jungle, and you've just passed a tiny village of Lacandón Indians on the right... that footpath is the trail to Bonampak, as unmarked as you please. At this writing the Lacandóns are clearing a patch of forest to the right of the trail, planning to build a store there, so there's no telling what you'll find there when you arrive; maybe nothing. If you continue on the gravel road past the cut-off to Bonampak, in about ten minutes you come to a small stream spanned by a log bridge, signaling that you've walked too far.

If you arrive at the trail head in a car and feel uncomfortable about leaving your vehicle unattended beside the road, speak to the Lacandón folk in Bethel, about 500 meters back up the road on which you've just come; go to the first hut on the left. If you offer a proper *gratificación* you may park your vehicle right in front of this hut.

I understand the hesitation you might experience about plunging into the jungle on an unmarked trail, so here are some more remarks about the trail, just to bolster your confidence. At the trail head, right where it meets the gravel road, you'll find black charcoal on the ground, from past campfires. If you pass down the trail for 30 or 50 meters, you'll pass two areas that have been cleared with machetes. *Cumbe* drivers from Palenque park in these shady spots waiting for their passengers to hike to the ruins and back. More than a few campers have pegged tents in these clearings, too.

After walking on the footpath for about two hours and fifteen minutes (about 10km) you'll come to a spacious grassy area in which permanent barracks and huts stand, and a tower with no antenna on it. This is the archeologist camp, where Bonampak's custodians stay.

If you've been looking for a spot "deep in the jungle" that you can comfortably use as a base as you bird-watch and generally wander around exploring the forest... this is it! If your *gratificaciones* generously reflect an understanding of how difficult it is to maintain such a camp so far from any regular town or paved road, and what an effort it takes to keep the camp attractive for visitors and bring in necessities from the outside, you'll certainly be welcome to stay for several days. On an unofficial, friend-to-friend basis, the custodians and their families will even provide food and other services. Of course, all it will take is a few freeloading visitors to ruin this situation for us all.

Other Options

Trails course all through the forest around Bonampak; in fact, one of the most interesting possibilities here is to hire a guide (speak with the custodians; usually there's a *chiclero* around) and hike all the way to Lagos de Montebello, about 100 air-kilometers (62mi) to the southwest.

One very fine "jungle walk" is to the nearby Río Lacanhá. It's about 45 minutes down a trail so frequently used that even the hiker with only average experience probably won't get lost. Of course, if you do get lost in this area, it'll be a deadly mistake. If you hike the trail to the Río Lacanhá, don't take a single step unless you know beyond all doubt that the trail you're leaving behind is so obvious that, when you return, you'll have no trouble at all following it back. As you're going in, follow your general progress with a compass.

To find where the trail to the Río Lacanhá leaves the ruins, just ask any of the custodians to point it out; it's between the camp and the ruin. Ask, "*¿Puede usted indicarme donde está el camino que va al Río Lacanhá, por favor?*"

Another interesting trip is to the ruin of Lacanhá, guided by a Lacandón Indian. To arrange this, go to Bethel, where most of the people are Lacandón converts to Seventh Day Adventism. Entering the village from the road, in the hut on the right, you may spot one of my friends, Sr Antonio Navarro, a near-albino Lacandón. This man will be your friend forever if you give him some vitamin pills! Two men in this village have told me they're willing to guide — Sr José Mallorca, the chief's son, and another friend of mine, Sr. Hidalgo González Chankín. Both men are real Lacandón, with long, black hair and flowing white tunics. The men have indicated that they'd expect US$20 or so for a day of guiding.

Curassow (Atlantic slope and south-east)

BIBLIOGRAPHY

General Traveling

Bicycling Mexico, by Ericka Weisbroth & Eric Ellman; 1990; Hunter Publishing, Inc., Edison, New Jersey. Distributed in Europe by Bradt Publications.

Mexico (4th edition), by Brosnahan et al; 1992; Lonely Planet, Australia.

A Guide to Ancient Maya Ruins, revised ed., by C. Bruce Hunter; 1986; University of Oklahoma Press; Norman, Oklahoma.

Let's Go Mexico, by Harvard Student Agency, Inc; updated yearly; St. Martin's Press; New York.

Mexico & Central American Handbook, edited by Ben Box; Trade & Travel Publications; Bath, England. Distributed in the U.S. by Rand McNally.

Mexico's Volcanoes: A Climbing Guide by R J Secor, published by The Mountaineers at 1011 S.W. Klickitat Way, Suite 107, Seattle, WA 98134 in 1981. In the U.S. you can order toll-free by phone at (800) 553-4453. This guide provides good climbing information and maps of six of Mexico's highest peaks. Unfortunately the author used his own car for access to most of the climbing areas and the book fails to detail methods of getting to the peaks by public transport.

Regional Guides

Baja California
The Baja Adventure Book by Walt Peterson. Wilderness Press. $16.95.

Baja California by Scott Wayne, Lonely Planet.

Baja California by W.W. Johnson, Time-Life Books, 1972.

Baja Explorer — Topographic Atlas Directory, Alti Publishing. In the U.S. call (800) 669-2252. 619-793-1704.

Into a Desert Place by Graham Mackintosh, Graham Mackintosh

Publishing, P. O. Box 1196, Idyllwild, CA 92549, 1990. In the US send $24.95 for a signed copy. Also available in the UK, £14.95, from Bradt Publications.

The Log from the Sea of Cortez by John Steinbeck, Penguin, 1977.

Magnificent Peninsula by Jack Williams, $14.95.

Baja California by Joe Cummings. Moon Publications 1992.

Northern Mexico

Trails of the Sierra Madre by Eugene Boudreau, Capra Press, California, 1973. A beautiful book describing various horseback trips taken with a guide in northwestern Mexico during the early 1970's. Backpackers could probably plan their own trips with this book's help. Excellent background information on the area's Indians, flora and fauna.

Copper Canyon

Copper Canyon - Barranca del Cobre by Richard D. Fisher and Luis G. Verplancken, Sunracer Publications, Tucson, AZ, 1991.

Mexico's Copper Canyon Country (A Hiking and Backpacking Guide to Tarahumara Land) by John Fayhee. Cordillera Press Inc., PO Box 3699, Evergreen, CO 80439. This is a comprehensive guide to trails starting from Creel and Batópilas. It costs US$12.95 from the publishers and is also available at the Mission Store and one or two other shops in Creel.

Guide to Mexico's Copper Canyon. $7.95 from Gordon Publishing, 91A Jane Ann, Campbell, CA 95008, USA.

National Geographic magazine of May, 1976 carries a feature on the Tarahumara Indians supported by beautiful photographs.

Among useful information available from the Hotel Santa Anita in Los Mochis are fold-out brochures prepared by Balderrama Hotels and Tours, containing interesting information on the trees of Barranca del Cobre. The entry lists 24 tropical dry-season, deciduous species and 9 tropical, river-bottom species.

Volcanos and National Parks

National Parks of Northwest Mexico, Volume II, by Rick Fisher, Sunracer Publications, PO Box 40092, Tuscon, AZ 85717. Superb photographs make this more a general-interest book than a serious guide for backpackers. It does however list short descriptions of a number of hikes. It costs US$11.95 and is also available at the Creel Mission Store.

Books on Mexico are available from Karll Franger Books, 3080 McBride Avenue, Surrey, BC Canada V4A 3HI. Other guide books and maps are available from Bradt Publications, 41 Nortoft Road, Chalfont St Peter, Bucks SL9 0LA. Send for a catalogue.

OTHER BOOKS ON SOUTH AMERICA FROM BRADT PUBLICATIONS

Backpacking and Trekking in Peru and Bolivia by Hilary Bradt
Fifth edition (1990) The classic guide for walkers and nature lovers.

Backpacking in Chile and Argentina (second edition)
Spectacular mountain scenery, well-run national parks, excellent food and wine, good transportation and safe cities. A hiker's and traveller's paradise.

No Frills Guide to Venezuela by Hilary Dunsterville Branch
Second edition. Venezuela offers uncrowded beaches and good snorkelling, splendid mountain walks and a variety of national parks. Also included is a detailed guide to Caracas, and different options for exploring the Angel Falls area.

South American River Trips by Tanis and Martin Jordan.
How to explore the rivers of South America in your own boat. Full of anecdote and humour, as well as information.

Backcountry Brazil by Alex Bradbury.
Three areas are covered in depth: Amazonia, the Pantanal, the north-east coast.

Climbing and Hiking in Ecuador (second edition) by Rob Rachowiecki and Betsy Wagenhauser.
New (1991) edition updated by the manager of the South American Explorer's Club in Quito.

Plus maps of every Latin American country.

This is just a selection of the books and maps for adventurous travellers that we stock. Send for our latest catalogue.

Bradt Publications, 41 Nortoft Rd, Chalfont St Peter, Bucks SL9 0LA, England. Tel: 0494 873478.

INDEX OF PLACES